A must-read book! [Toby is] an awesome man of God who loves his family and friends. [He's] a great friend of mine who has such a servant's heart. A wonderful inspiration to us.

Lisa, Nashville, TN

Over the years, I have seen a beautiful relationship grow between Toby and his daughters, Bria and Lexy. They will always have memories to cherish about their daddy–daughter dates and the times he has played little girl games with them. He seemed to truly understand how much it would mean to them as they grew older. Some times it must have been tough for this big, six foot two man. He must have wanted to play football and manly games, but he allowed himself to be a big teddy bear whenever these two little angels needed some time with their daddy. I can honestly say that I am so thankful and proud of my son and my daughter-in-law because they have done well in their parenting journey and they can be very thankful because they have two girls that love the Lord and have a huge desire to serve him. What a blessing!

Sherry, Jackson, MI

This is a hilarious, yet true account of what a stay-at-home father will encounter. Based on Christian principles, this book is a must-read for parents or grandparents. The true-to-life experience related in this book will shed light on parenting and bring a smile to your face.

Debbie, Hendersonville, TN

Daddy

do my **socks** match?

Daddy
do my **socks** match?

Adventures of a Stay-At-Home Dad

Toby J. Swager

Tate Publishing & *Enterprises*

Published by Tate Publishing & Enterprises, LLC
127 E. Trade Center Terrace | Mustang, Oklahoma 73064 USA
1.888.361.9473 | www.tatepublishing.com

Tate Publishing is committed to excellence in the publishing industry. The company reflects the philosophy established by the founders, based on Psalm 68:11,
"The Lord gave the word and great was the company of those who published it."

Cover design by Summer Harvey
Interior design by Amber Lee

Published in the United States of America

ISBN: 978-1-60696-585-6
1. Religion: Christianity: Christian Life-Family
2. Christian Living: Relationships: Parenting

08.11.18

Dedication

This book is dedicated to those individuals who realize what an awesome blessing and responsibility raising a child and being a parent really is. It is for parents, grand-parents and everyone in between. You can make a lasting impact on this world by being the best mom or dad you can be. I hope the words within bring you encouragement to follow God's plan for your life. God bless.

Acknowledgements

The nine years of parenthood that inspired this book have had times of struggle and times of bliss. Along the way, there have been many people who have helped me and my wife rise to meet the challenge of raising our children. Family members and friends have influenced and encouraged us to be the best parents we can be. We are extremely grateful to those who have been there for us spiritually and emotionally.

I would like to say thank you to all of my family and friends, but there are too many to name here. You have each touched my life in unique ways and have helped me to better understand what family is all about. Thank you, Dad, Mo, Grandma Swager, Grandma and Grandpa Litchard, Grandpa File, Jimmy and Jennifer, Mom, Kenny, and Mom and Dad Hilton. I love you all.

I would like to express a special thank you to my mom, who inspired me to consider writing about my experiences with my girls. Thank you for your help and support.

A special thank you to the following: Sherry and Kenny Williams, Karen Beers, Dawn Casey, Marilyn Wilson, Bryant Bickel, Mary Jacobs, Chuck Spidle, Greg and Sara Owens, John Driver, Rick and Jenny Morris, John and Emily Bannach, Janet and Daniel McElhiney, Mark and Joanie Lee Stewart, Debbie Graves and Teri Clark; without your support and prayers, this book would not be possible.

Thank you to Pastor Darin. You are a great friend and mentor. And to my church family, thanks for supporting my dream. Thank you, Chris and Shannon Brown, for being there for my family; you guys are great. Thank you to all the students and parents who make up Heartburn Youth Ministries; your prayers have helped strengthen me.

Most of all, thank you to my two beautiful girls, Bria and Lexy. Being your dad is a privilege. I will always be proud of you! To my wife, Tracy; I love you! We have two great kids and I thank God everyday that he brought us together. Thank you for being the perfect partner for me.

And to my Savior; thank you for loving me when I was unlovable. Thank you, God, for giving me the gift of being a parent and for having a plan for my life.

Table of Contents

Foreword

Hi! My name is Tracy Swager, and I am not a stay-at-home parent. My husband is, and here's my perspective on it.

When I got pregnant with our first child, Bria, in 1998, I began doing child-care research. I was appalled at the cost of child-care for a week. I found it was going to cost us $100 to $150 per week for someone to watch our baby while we were working. That was not an exciting thought. (Don't get me wrong, here. Excellent child care is worth the price. But it sure hurts the family budget!)

As I moved along in my pregnancy, I actually ventured out to look at a child-care facility. I found one right down the road from our house, and it was only $80 per week. A pastor's wife managed the facility. The building was old, but inside it was clean. I was impressed by the ratio of children to staff. We began to look at our budget.

When we sat down and put all of our expenses on paper, added in child care and looked at what we thought our income would do in the coming months, I was even less excited. It was depressing for me to think about paying all that money for someone else to watch our child. Plus, with our work hours, I was a little worried about making it to the daycare by 6:00 p.m. and avoiding by-the-minute late fees. I thought we had no choice.

I believe it was Toby's idea first. He had the revolutionary thought of his staying home. At first I thought there was no way it could work. But, we went back to our budget. Since I have a college degree, I was making more than my husband. So, we moved our numbers around and took the estimated child care expenses out of his paycheck. In essence, he would have been working for only a few dollars an hour.

Then, we started to look hard at the possibility of Toby staying home to care for our baby. We took his income out of the budget. We made sure expenses like diapers and formula were added. Bria was due in November. A month later, our car would be paid off. That would be another $300 per month. For the first time, I began to get excited. It actually looked possible. We committed to keeping our child at home. Our baby would spend her nights *and days* being cared for by one of her parents.

Looking back, the Lord certainly led our decision-making process–it was clearly the right choice for our family. It may not be the right choice for everyone, but it was for us. Now, it wasn't always easy… there were some challenges!

For one, my husband and I had to lay down our assumptions about male and female roles. That took getting over some pride–on both of our parts! The good news about that–I discovered that a daddy can actually live through changing a diaper. Toby lived through hundreds of them!

Seriously, having my husband stay home was wonderful, but I had to adjust. I had moments where I fought jealousy over some of the things my husband experienced with our children while I was at work. Not the diapers, mind you, but other wonderful moments. The LORD taught me that we both had to be intentional about building a relationship with our kids.

I also had to get over the fact that my husband wouldn't do things just like me. I wasn't always successful in crushing that critical spirit, but it's important that I worked on that. My husband needs my support–at whatever God calls him to do. When he let the girls pick their own clothes, running around in pink t-shirts and bright green tights, I needed to step back and enjoy the humor of the sight. Sometimes I just have to relax.

We also had to learn how to deal with the criticism of others. Not everyone agreed with our decision of Toby staying home. He was subtly (and sometimes not-so-subtly) offered correction (and criticism) by many men in our lives. So many don't understand what it means to walk by faith–to do what God has so clearly spoken to you even when it doesn't make sense. We had to deal with attacks on his self-esteem because some of those men around us only found their value in the amount of their paycheck. That's a sad life, isn't it? Let me say this clearly–there are so many things a husband and father has a responsibility to provide for his family. The least of these things is money. God has provided all of our needs, and my husband has been faithful to his call to love me as Christ loved the church and to teach our children God's way. That is true success as a husband and father–success that many we know will never see without a dramatic change in their hearts. Make no mistake. That change only comes through faith in Jesus Christ.

Yes, I'm grateful that my husband was a stay-at-home dad for five years. My girls have a relationship with their daddy that most do not. They know they are adored, protected and held accountable. When the time comes, they know to expect respect from a boy–because their daddy taught them on daddy-daughter dates. They know *both* their parents will always be there for them, and, most importantly, they know what it is to walk a life of faith before the LORD. Yes, I'm grateful indeed.

Introduction

I have two lovely children, and I wouldn't trade my experiences with them for anything. So I don't have a fancy car or a big home; the status symbols of this world are fleeting and can be bought and sold. I have something greater than all the things of this world, something that cannot be purchased; it will not change over time. I have made an investment that has a higher rate of return than any mutual fund could dream of reporting. I have given my love, and I have been overwhelmed by the experiences that I have enjoyed. I have memories that will outlast the best car on the road, and for that, I am thankful. What more could a man ask for?

I'm a Stay–At-Home Dad

"Hi! My name is Toby and I'm a stay–at-home dad."

Let's face it, sometimes that's how you feel. The worst part of staying home isn't the diapers—you'll get used to the smell. It's not even the crying (yours or the child's). It's your pride.

You're at a gathering with people you know and some you don't and everyone begins talking about what they do. At first, I felt that being a volunteer youth pastor, an online entrepreneur (you wouldn't believe how much you can make selling stuff from yard sales on eBay), a jack-of-all-trades odd job man and a stay-at-home dad wasn't good enough. When the conversation came to this point, I would assume that no matter what was said, each person in the room would gather and discuss how lazy I was.

Of course, that was a completely unreasonable conclusion to reach. Most people were impressed by the sacrifice (yes, I said sacrifice) of a man who was willing to do whatever was necessary to help his family make it. Very few people looked at me as lazy, and most of the ones who did, didn't know me. They were unaware of the numerous cars I worked on for friends. They didn't know that I would do little fix-it jobs here and there or that I would mow lawns for people in the neighborhood. I would sell CD's, books, clothing, anything of value to someone on internet auction sites. I would even work part-time for a sign company when work was available. On top of that, I was volunteering on staff at our church and caring for our girls. Sure, I wasn't bringing in a phenomenal amount of cash, but I was providing for my family. Lazy? Far from it.

Still, I would spend hours fighting the feeling that people were looking down on us, me in particular. And there were probably some who were, but not nearly the number of my imaginings. What I was fighting more than anything was my pride. No matter how well we were doing, it was never good enough. We never did without. We always had food, clothing, a roof over our heads and transportation that was reliable most of the time, but I still felt like I was somehow failing my family.

I would try to figure out a way in which mine and my wife's roles could be reversed. She had the college degree and the God-given job, and I had a lot of abilities, but no degree. I believe God used this time in our lives to humble me. You see, I knew in and of myself that I was capable of anything. This is not pride—this is knowing your limits, and I knew God had given me the ability to fix things that I had no idea how they worked. I knew that God had given me the ability to build things with minimal experience at carpentry. He had given me the ability to look at something, know what it did and how to dismantle and put it back together so that it worked properly. All those skills are a great asset as a youth pastor or in the ministry field in general, but I still hadn't accepted the direction God was leading me. I still believed that God had something different in store for me. It didn't even occur to me that I had all these abilities and skills because he had called me to help build young lives.

When I realized what was happening and I finally let go and let God have control, I was able to look back and see where he had been directing us all along. I had let the mutterings of a few and the perceived ideas of what should be in the eyes of society to convince me that I was a failure. If I had continued looking at myself in that light, I don't know what would have become of me or my family. Thankfully, God put people in my path who helped to quiet the voices of condemnation, imagined and real. They helped me to realize that I had been putting far too much value in what others thought of me, that I had been over-analyzing conversations and things people would say, instead of focusing on what God was and had been doing in our lives. Without the help of my wife, my pastor, my family and friends, I would have given up long before the fight ever started.

When I saw how God was moving, I was amazed.

The Bible says in Proverbs 20:24, "A man's steps are directed by the LORD. How then can anyone understand his own way?" (NIV) When I looked back over my life, I was awestruck at how true that scripture is. He brought us from Michigan to Tennessee, where we basically knew no one except an uncle who lived in Nashville and Tracy's mom and dad an hour away. He used a radio personality to direct us. He provided a great job for my wife that laid the ground work for her to do what she is doing now. He provided me the training and opportunity I needed to become a pastor in the Assembly of God church. He had a network in place and all we had to do was trust in his plan and believe that he knew what he was doing. Even writing this book has been in his plan, and he has used numerous methods to encourage me to keep going when I felt like giving up. Naturally, there would be opposition to his plan for my life. If it were easy, then I would doubt that we were in his plan.

There are many reasons you might find yourself in a role-reversal. Maybe the company you have worked for has downsized, and you were a victim of restructuring. Maybe you injured yourself, and your wife is working to help make ends meet. Maybe God is trying to teach you something. No matter the reason, trust him. You are no less of a man because you are changing diapers than you would be if you were changing the gaskets on a cylinder head. You are providing a valuable service to your family as well as society, so don't give up. Don't listen to the nay-sayers; follow the leading of God for your life.

This book isn't intended to convince you to make the same choices my wife and I did. Each situation is unique. Every family faces trials, and though they might seem similar from a distance, they are specific to the people who make up that family. You may be called on to be a caregiver and work part-time. You may be a full-time employee, a business owner or you might stay home with your kids and work odd jobs when opportunities arise. Regardless, you are a father to your children.

I believe every man has the blueprint of being a father inside because we are all created in the image of the perfect Father. There is so much more to being a dad than bringing home a paycheck each week. Making more than your wife is not the issue. It is more important that you be there for your children. They won't always come to you but they will know you are there for them. Whether you are a stay-at-home dad or you work full-time, you are a husband and father first and whatever else you may be comes second.

I would hope that all men would find use from the information in this book rather than overlooking it just because it was written to help fathers who stay home with their children. I believe the Lord has inspired a great deal of the ideas within. Without his guidance, I do not believe you would be holding it in your hands right now. He has ordered your steps, he knew you in your mother's womb and he knows you still. Trust him; he won't lead you astray.

Deciding To Be a Stay-At-Home Dad

When I think about how my wife, Tracy, and I came to be in this situation, one thing comes to mind: money. When we discovered that we would be having a baby soon, we were excited and scared. We would sit down and discuss how our lives would be different. How would we manage? Would we be able to afford it? Would this bring us closer together as a couple, or drive us apart?

Well, we have managed and continue to do so. You take things as they come. You will struggle, you will question your own sanity, but those are some of the many joys of parenting! Yes, your life will be different. It will be blessed. Don't let those people who you will undoubtedly encounter tell you how much your life will change. Your life changes everyday, you make changes and go on, end of story. Don't look at this miracle that God has given as something that will change you so much that two years down the road you won't be able to recognize yourself. That will lead to resentment, and that is why so many marriages today fail. Let's face it - if you and your wife aren't ready for the changes that you will go through, in 99% of all cases, it's your own fault. Except for the ignorant few who don't know where babies come from, you have no excuse.

Let's get back to our discussions. Would we be able to afford it? If we had waited until it was more convenient, I wouldn't be writing this. If you wait until you can afford to have a child, you will never have a child. Plain and simple, for most families in the United States, having a child will put a strain on your finances. Wait, don't throw this book away just yet; I'm telling you like it is. You will encounter new expenses, for your baby and yourself. The good thing is this: you will learn how to make things last longer.

For any family that is considering a role-reversal, or a "Mr. Mom" situation, talk it through. Sit down and write things out on paper. How will things be different? What are you or your spouse willing to give up in your life? What are you not willing to give up? If you're not willing to give up more than you're unwilling to give up, you shouldn't be having a child to begin with because you are selfish.

When Tracy and I first started talking about the changes we would encounter, we wondered how we would afford daycare. We questioned if we wanted someone who we didn't know what they believed in having as much if not more influence over our child than we would. Then, we began to figure finances before and after the baby would be born. We came to the very real and very scary realization that if I continued working after, it would be to pay for someone else to raise our child. When we realized this, we started to panic. We felt like we were ready emotionally for the task of child-rearing, but we knew that we had made a mistake because we didn't have financial stability. We got scared, and we argued some. We prayed, then we argued some more. We were looking at this as an inconvenience, not a blessing.

I think Tracy realized that fact first. As the day drew nearer, and as we began to think more rationally, we began to listen as we prayed. It really didn't take as long as it sounds. We had made our decision that I would stay home and care for the baby before the fifth month of pregnancy. I still struggled though, wondering, *Am I making the right decision? Will this really work?* These fears were echoed by many people and added to my own apprehension. Family members and friends questioned our judgment and told us that our marriage wouldn't survive.

The real problem I encountered was pride. I would think, *I am the man, I shouldn't be doing this.* I was providing for my family, but I couldn't see that. All I could see were dollar signs and things that I wanted for us to have that we wouldn't be able to afford. I wasn't able to accept and abide by the plan God had for me and my family until I humbled myself. It doesn't matter what others say or think. If we stray from the design that God has for us, we are no longer serving him, but serving man. We are putting the thoughts and judgments of the world before the command of God, and that is sin.

It wasn't like I was going to be sitting at home eating bon bons and doing nothing. I was a volunteer youth pastor at the time and knew that God was pulling me from the secular work place into the ministry. This provided an opportunity to grow in the Lord and in ministry, all the while sharing it with my kids. It gave me more time to focus on students and developing a plan to excel. Besides, when God speaks to us, he generally tells us what he wants us to do. Some times he will use others, but typically he will speak directly to us, if we'll listen. What he says doesn't always make sense to everyone and that is where faith comes in. We had to trust him, and we did.

Family and Friends

As you can imagine, being a stay-at-home dad isn't all fun and games. People who you trust to understand and be there for you seem to disappear. You are sometimes greeted with scorn and disapproval. We were told how much we were harming our girls. It can be disheartening, but don't get me wrong; this book isn't about bashing those people, they thought that they were helping. They just didn't have all the facts.

You see, each instance is different. Each family is unique. Though there may be similarities in families across America, each unit is made up of individuals who bring different skills and personality traits to the marriage. The most important part of any family unit is the marriage. The husband and wife relationship is intended to last long after the children have left the nest. It is the job of each married couple to know the strengths and weaknesses of their partner, not so they have ammunition for fights down the road, but so they can truly be one in every situation.

The people who told us how we were hurting our kids have since remarked on how impressed they were with their behavior. They have stated that they didn't know how we did it, but whatever we did worked. Now not everyone who felt we were wrong for the choices we made has come back to us and said these things, but many have.

You have to understand. The people who tell you you'll regret your choices in the long run are looking at the situation from their own perspective. For them, it might be true that their marriage wouldn't survive or that they would be ruining their kids lives.

For me and my wife, it came down to doing what we had to do to survive. It was a little awkward at times, but we managed, because we knew each other's strengths, we leaned on them, and, over time, were strengthened in our relationship because we had learned to depend on each other.

You don't have to prove your manliness by working excessive hours to see to it that people accept you. If you put your family at risk because you want others to accept your choices, then you have made the wrong decision. Here's the thing. Some people will look down on you. So what? They couldn't see themselves in your situation. Big deal. I am who I am whether they like me or not. Some people just won't like you; some people won't respect you, and that's their problem. You have to make your decisions based on what's best for your family, not the opinions of those around you.

When it's all said and done, you are responsible for the decisions you make. Listen to the advice of elders. In most instances, they aren't trying to hurt you. However, the choice is yours and your wife's. No one else knows what's best for your family. And try as they may, they won't be able to make sense of your choices and that's okay. Don't be bitter! Don't hold it against those people. Be encouraged that they love you enough to share their personal feelings with you. Realize that they are speaking from their own perspective and could never see things as you do. It can be very easy to become prideful and say something that you might regret later, so politely nod and move on with your life. Love them, love your wife and love your children as Christ loves us and you can't go wrong.

There is an old Indian adage that states, "Never judge a man until you have walked a mile in his moccasins." And in the Bible, we find, "Judge not, and ye shall not be judged" (Luke 6:37, KJV) Bitterness and pride lead to judgment. Thoughts like, *Who do they think they are telling me how to live?* or, *Well, I'll show them…* may momentarily encourage you. They may even help you make it through the next trial, but it won't last. Opinion is based on perspective; judgment is based on opinion. Understand that your opinions differ and respect one another. If you are still disrespected, understand that it is just their opinion, know in your heart where you stand and respect the other person's opinion; after all, everyone's got one.

If I had allowed the opinions of friends and family

to sway me from what my wife and I knew we were to do in our hearts, no matter how difficult it was, our marriage would have suffered. I would not be a youth pastor today. I don't believe I would have the respect for those people who shared their opinions that I do. And I don't believe my children would have had half the experiences they have had with Mom and Dad. And they are better for it.

So, seek out and follow God's plan for your family. Trust me, it's the best option. Maybe that plan includes being a stay-at-home dad, and maybe it doesn't. Remember this, though: if God has given you children, then you are a full-time father and have all the responsibility that goes with it. This responsibility includes teaching your children about the LORD, building a relationship with them, loving and protecting them. In these pages, you will find inspiration, encouragement, and instruction to be the best full-time father you can be.

Emotional Wreck

Whatever you do as a father, do not make the mistake of hiding your emotions from your children. We as men have this perception that we have to be strong, and that means never being wrong or showing emotions that we perceive as weak. Think about it, guys. When was the last time you had a good, healthy cry? It is extremely important for your children to realize it is all right to have feelings.

For example, when we grieve, crying is a natural release. However, most men will hold back for the sake of showing strength and never properly complete the grieving process. Our children emulate the things they see in us. If they see us holding our pain inside, they will see this as the proper way to deal with grief, and they will never learn how to truly let go of their pain.

We as fathers need to let our children know how much we love them. We expect a five-year-old to know that we love them by the things we do for them. Is it any wonder so many people find it hard to believe that their Father in heaven loves them no matter what? I remember the first time I held our oldest daughter. It was incredible, this new life I held in my hands; what a privilege to be a dad. What an awesome responsibility. The moment she was born, there was this overwhelming love inside for this beautiful little girl. She wasn't very clean, but she was beautiful. At that moment, I would have died for her to live. I made a commitment to God, to my wife and to myself, that no matter what, I would tell her how much she meant to me.

It was really quite funny. I held her before my wife. Sorry, but I did. Those first twenty-four hours, the only time she was out of my sight was when they had to take her for medical reasons. I carried her to her first bath, where they weighed her and measured her. I did the same thing for our second. The hospital you use may not be so willing to bend the rules, but ours was. Those were important moments in that little girl's life, and I was going to be there whether she remembered it or not. Someone needed to be able to share it with my wife who was recovering. (She was fine; she wanted me to go, and I would have been back at her side in a second if she needed me.)

I don't know if that attitude is what has made it so important to me that my children know they are loved. I have cried while punishing them (Dad, I understand now, it really does hurt me more). I have cried when they had success and when they have experienced failure. In each instance, I assure them that they are loved, and I will always be proud of them no matter what.

I want them to know that their value doesn't come from the grades on a report card or the interests they share with me; their value is the same whether they are in trouble or they just recited their latest memory verse. And if I love them this much, how much more does God love them? He gave his own Son; I don't think I could do that, maybe I could, but I don't know.

Your love will be the foundation of every relationship that your child has throughout life, boy or girl, period. There confidence comes from knowing that they are loved by you. They will look for a spouse who has similar qualities and values. "Train a child in the way he should go, and when he is old he will not turn from it" (Proverbs 22:6, NIV) is not just a bunch of fluff. They will succeed at work, at school and at life, and it all comes back to your relationship with them. I told you it was an awesome responsibility!

Now, on occasion, someone will surpass and exceed their upbringing, but that is very difficult. True, each individual is responsible for the choices they make, and Mommy or Daddy not loving them enough is a pretty pitiful excuse for poor choices. More often than not, it's just a bad choice. But don't depend on your child to understand that you work because you love them or you gave them a roof over their head because you love them. Kids need tangible love; they need to know that you hurt when they hurt, not because you say so, but because they see it in you.

Show your child you love them by sacrificing your wants and desires for them. Allow them to be what God wants them to be. Guide them and direct them. Make it a point to be there for that school play; maybe you won't be able to buy them as much for Christmas, but the memory of seeing your face in the crowd will never go away. Then you will be that hero they've always seen you as.

Give 'Em Lots of Love

I am a very emotional man. The world looks at this as weakness, but I feel it's just the opposite. It is a sign of strength. God gave us emotions to strengthen us, not weaken us. Do not hesitate to express yourself emotionally to your children. You will be the example that will mold their lives. How they handle relationships and how they raise their own children will be based on what they see you do in the same situations.

I have heard many men make excuses when it comes to expressing their love for their kids. We allow our past to keep us from doing things like saying, "I love you," or hugging our children. We have to overcome our own childhood as a parent. We have the divine example of our Father in heaven who loved us enough to allow his Son to die for us. As a father, you have to make it a priority to tell your children that you love them. Don't assume that they know just because you provide a roof over their head or food for their belly; those things are wonderful, but they don't show a child that you love them. Express yourself. Spend time with them. It amazes me that we can think a four-year-old child would put a higher value on a bed to sleep in than a loving touch from a parent.

Think about it: if you grew up without hearing "I love you" or feeling an embrace from your father, you craved it. Don't encourage your kids to misbehave by withholding your emotions and only showing love through discipline. A good measure of this is do you tend to say things like, "This hurts me more than it will hurt you," more than, "I love you?" Discipline has its place, but discipline is pointless if you do not have the love and respect of the one being disciplined, and it is hard for a child to accept that discipline if they don't feel your love more frequently than your wrath.

If you have daughters, take them out on a "date-with-daddy," and show them how a man should treat a woman. Have a son? Show interest in things that interest him, don't force your own likes on him. If you show interest in what he likes, most often, he will show an interest in you.

This cannot be overstressed. Tell your children you love them. Don't say, "Well, that's just not how I was raised." That is a cop-out. Make peace with your past, and tell your children you love them. Break the cycle. Make a difference in the lives of your children.

We all look at this country and how it has changed in just a short time. We are so busy with providing things for our kids that many times a family is never together in one place, Mother, Father and children all at one time. The sad thing is that our pursuit of more things takes us away from the ones who need us most. You having that new car or the perfect house doesn't help your kids, it hurts them.

Ever wonder why, when a child receives a present, more often than not, they are more excited about the box than about what is inside? There are two ways to look at this. Children don't need to have the fanciest stuff to be happy. Simple things please a child more than all the high-tech gadgets in this world. Maybe living a little more modestly would simplify our own lives in a way that would make us more available.

My girls would much rather pick a tickle-fight with Daddy than have Daddy gone all day just so they can have a bigger house. I think about times I spent at the park with them that built an irreplaceable relationship. Houses crumble, cars rust, and money has a way of disappearing, but you will always have the relationships that you develop with your children.

My Beautiful Wife

(She Can Go from Smile to Cry in 5.2 Seconds)

When my wife and I discovered that we were pregnant, I thought I was ready for everything. I expected the obvious signs, but my wife went through physical and emotional changes that I wasn't prepared for. There was nothing to prepare me for the things she experienced. We went to classes and, though they made mention of physical changes, they didn't even touch the reality of the situation. I read the books, some with my wife and some without, but even that didn't prepare me for what was to come.

She experienced cravings. Her tastes changed. She became obsessed with cleaning house. Truth be told, there were some things that were nice. I was no less attracted to her while she was pregnant and the nesting instinct was great! (The girls and I do most of the house work; sometimes I long for the days of pregnancy.)

For me, the changes were external. Some were

peculiar, some were funny, but at most they were a minor inconvenience. I had no idea the physical and emotional stress she was experiencing. Yes, I questioned whether or not I would be a good father. I contemplated the impact that this new life would have on our marriage, our family. I was awed by the awesome miracle and intimidated by the responsibility that God had placed on me when he chose to allow me to be a father. Even with that, it didn't come close to the strain my wife had undergone. She was carrying this new life, experiencing the changes the baby went through while struggling with the changes she was going through.

Where I wondered, *Will I be a good dad?* she was wondering, *Am I a good mother?* When I would contemplate, *How will this affect our family?* she would question, *Will he still love me if I never lose all this weight?* There were more questions in her mind than I ever could have imagined, and they were all very real concerns. The emotional impact of carrying a life for nine months is huge.

As a man, some of the things she would say or think seemed ridiculous. The times she would say, "I'm fat," I would think, *Well, duh, you've got the equivalent of a Thanksgiving turkey rolling around inside you!* And though it was quite funny to watch her trying to get out of bed sometimes, in her mind it wasn't; at least, not every time.

You see, something that was funny to her one day could be quite upsetting the next. We would laugh together, and I would tell her she looked like a turtle that had flipped over and couldn't turn upright when she couldn't get out of bed, and most times she thought it just as funny as I did. I would come and help her get sat up and then help her stand and she would playfully slap at me, but, some days she would cry. Not because I hurt her feelings (I didn't even say it every time) but because she was so overwhelmed by the experience.

I remember asking her one day, "Honey, why are you crying? Are you okay? Do you need something? Want a chicken sandwich from Burger King (one of her cravings)?" I will never forget what she said to me. It was kind of funny, but it helped me to understand where she was at in that moment. She said, "I don't know why I'm crying. Nothing's wrong, I just feel like crying. I'm not hungry. I don't need you to do anything. I just want you to hold me." So I did. We would sit and talk for hours sometimes and I would tell her how happy I was that we were going to experience this miracle together. I would talk to the baby through her belly button (seemed like the logical place to me). I would sing to her and stroke her hair and be there for her, whether we were crying together or laughing. I was there.

Seriously now, dads and future dads, this isn't something you can fix. I know you want to solve every problem. If she would tell you what she needed, you would find it. Relax! She doesn't need you to do or fix or repair anything. She just needs you to understand. If she wants to cry, let her cry. Cry with her! Be real and let her know that she's not alone. Share your thoughts with her and really listen to hers. Hold her and tell her that you love her. Tell her that you love your child. Tell her how happy you are to share this experience with her. Be there for her!

One thing you do need to be aware of is the reality of postpartum depression. It isn't something to take lightly and it doesn't just go away. No one knows your wife better than you. If you sense anything unusual beyond the normal process of recovery, don't hesitate to address it. Be compassionate. Your wife just went through one of the most traumatic events a human being can endure. She will be different for a time. She will need to heal physically and emotionally, but if, three months after the birth of your child, she is still struggling, be man enough to address the situation, for your wife's and your own benefit.

If left untreated, postpartum depression can go on for years after childbirth. It affects each person differently and can even be hard to tell that that is what is going on. My wife and I didn't realize what she was experiencing until six years after our last child was born. We just thought she was too busy and didn't get enough exercise. When we finally talked about it, and I mean really discussed it, it became obvious. Don't let her bear that burden alone!

That said, be there for her. Stability goes a long way in the process of recovery. Tell her she is beautiful, that you still love her as much, even more than before. Tell her that nothing has changed. She needs to know that, despite everything that has changed about her, you still are willing to die for her. Yes, my wife became an emotional wreck. I had to be okay with that. It didn't make me a bad husband because I couldn't take the pain away or find the one perfect thing that would make it all better. Do what you can and let nature deal with the rest and be thankful you're not an elephant! They carry their children for over a year!

Me and My Shadow

One of the most awkward moments in the life of a child is when they discover their shadow. It was pretty amusing to me, but it was a time of uncertainty for my children. There was fear. There were questions like, "Why does it always follow me?" I decided to make some games to help the girls adapt to this ever-present companion. It helped them through their fear and uncertainty, and it was fun.

We would step on each other's shadows. I'm sure it looked a little weird, but it was fun. You would be surprised how difficult it can be to avoid having your shadow stepped on. Plus, it can be fun to shout, "Hey, you stepped on my shadow," while you're in the mall. You should try it some time.

We tried to hide from our shadows, which was much more difficult than stepping on a shadow. Those things will follow you everywhere! Even when you shut off the lights, they are there, lurking, just waiting for that light to return so they pop up beside you.

We dealt with all of the questions and fear and, eventually, the girls got comfortable with the fact that, no matter where they went, their shadow would be right there with them. I remember our oldest trying to hug her shadow and kiss her shadow. In fact, it became a source of great concern for me. How close do I let her get to this shadow character anyway? Who does he think he is? It's great practice for the dating years.

We would make different faces and we would try making shadow puppets on the wall. One such face was affectionately known as "kissy face." It was that face my children made when they were little that meant they wanted a kiss. If you have kids, you know the one. Lips puckered, drool and a little bit of whatever candy they were eating stuck trickling down their face, straining to kiss you while all you can think of is, *Yuck, I have no idea where that face has been!* Not my favorite kisses in the world, but they sure enjoyed giving them. They would laugh at me as I tried to contort my body into shapes I nearly got stuck in, just to avoid the kiss of my child. How ridiculous! I would eventually kiss them, and then as soon as they were out of sight, I would wipe the sticky combination of drool, food particles and some snot from my face and think how lucky I was to be so loved.

My oldest daughter came up with a shadowy game of her own. It was a little disconcerting and had nothing to do with shadows, but it was a little strange and frightening until I got used to it. At any given moment of any day, for no apparent reason, my daughter would shout "surprise." She would then inform me that we were having a party. I think it stemmed from a surprise party we threw for my wife when she was little. She loved that surprise party feeling so much, she decided for a time that we should enjoy it every day.

There were preparations to be made. There were parties planned that never came to pass, and then there were those days where she got everything right and at the shouting of the magic word, "surprise"; we were at a party. There were days in the middle of the week when my wife would come home and, for no apparent reason, it was a surprise party. It might have been just the three or four of us, depending on whether her sister were born or not, but the size of the party didn't matter; it was a celebration!

It was odd, but the parties stopped just as quickly as they began. I don't know if she forgot or if they just weren't as fun anymore, but the surprise surprise-parties, the kissy-face game and the shadow stepping all came to an end about the same time. Strangely, I was a little sad. They were soon replaced with tea parties and similar things, but I always wondered what happened to the little kissy-faced, shadow-stomping, surprise-party thrower. I guess they have to grow up, but we don't have to like it!

The Mind of a Child

A child's mind can be a very frightening place without reason or logic, filled with imaginary places and imaginary people. My oldest daughter had an imaginary friend appropriately named Friend. She used to pretend that she was a mother and that she had ten imaginary children who we would wait for as they got out of the car. It was stressful. I wanted to scream, "Get your lazy little imaginary kids outta the car so I can go inside Piggly Wiggly and buy myself a soda," but I didn't. It was hard, but I didn't.

My children have been an adventure that I hope never ends. There have been rollercoaster rides, haunted houses and the occasional death-defying leap of faith. Sometimes, I have had to step back and watch so that they could learn a valuable lesson on their own. At other times, I have gotten to save them from perilous decisions that could have grave consequences. No matter the situation, I have enjoyed this adventure known as parenthood. It's like a never-ending Choose-Your-Own-Adventure book; not every decision leads to life–or-death consequences, but they all affect the journey.

Every experience is an opportunity to create a memory. Those memories will last longer than that first bike or those incredible shoes they just have to have because everyone else does. You can set aside one million dollars for your child's future, but if you haven't created any memories, they will resent you for it. No amount of money can replace time spent with a child.

Act like an idiot, run and scream, play in the snow, do whatever it takes to impact their lives. My children like to make up plays; sometimes they are good, sometimes not so good, but I watch them, and they remember it. Whether it be a go-cart ride together or playing Barbies in the playroom, (not exactly my strongest area-we always end up racing in the Barbie cars or fighting some unknown evildoer, but we're making memories!) be enthusiastic and have fun. Let your kids see you act silly. It's okay, they won't think you're weird. They'll love you for it.

The Latest Fashion

"Hello. My name is Toby and I am a fashion coordinator."

What difference does it make if your socks match your shoes? Why can't you wear purple and lime green together with red and pink? It's all so confusing! Does it really matter if your pajamas match? And why is it necessary to match when you aren't going anywhere?

For me, the challenge wasn't that I couldn't tell what the colors were; I just didn't care. Who were we trying to impress? Apparently, there are fashion police all around us, we just don't realize it! What is the fine for wearing bright orange socks with white sandals and a green dress? Trust me, it's larger than you can imagine.

I discovered shortly after my daughters were born that my wife was a covert operative for the fashion police. I was fined many times for improper outfits or failing to make the girls change out of their pajamas. We weren't going anywhere, so what's the big deal?

The big deal is simply this: I am raising young ladies, not boys. Boys should match, but people don't think less of the parents when they don't. Girls are a different story. It was as if my wife felt that it reflected poorly on her when the girls' clothes didn't match. Through this, I discovered that it was more important to my wife than to the girls, and I have had lots of fun with it. However, if it's important to my wife, then it's important to me. (No, she isn't standing behind me as I write this!)

There are some things I would never do. I would never let my beautiful girls go to an important event without making sure that they have brushed their hair. I made this mistake once; never again! I will not allow them to dress themselves when we are going out without looking at the choices they made and correcting poor ones when necessary. I have been bitten in this area more than once. It never mattered to me that my NASCAR apparel wasn't coordinated at the races or that I mix team colors at a hockey game. Well, it never mattered to me before, but now…

I have begun making wardrobe decisions for myself based on where we are going and what we will be doing there. Shorts are not always the appropriate attire. When I go to a sporting event, I wear clothes that are sport-appropriate, meaning I don't wear my favorite drivers gear to a college football game. How uncivilized would that be? It gets worse!

I have caught myself thinking things like, *How could they wear that to the convenience store*, or, *Their mother should really help them get dressed in the morning. Baby blue and pink, together, disgusting!* Oh, there's more!

I used to check my clothing choices with my wife on a regular basis. Now I can dress myself and, typically, I find no need to consult my wife on the finer points of outfit preparation. It scares me. I have even been shopping with the girls and said no to a shirt because we couldn't find just the right shade of blue to accent the flowers in the shirt. (We were shopping for the girls, not for me!)

Now when we go out, I look at the clothes the girls have chosen, and I say things I never thought I would hear myself say. "You can't wear that color hair bow with those pants." "You need to change that or we aren't leaving this house!" I have even said, "Did you get dressed in the dark or something because those socks aren't even close to matching. One's salmon and the other is just plain pink! Go change that before your mother sees you."

Now, it's not a bad thing. I know that it is important to match and I could probably advise in most situations. There is the occasional time where I defer to their mother, but, for the most part, I can dress myself. I can tell the girls whether they have made a good choice or a bad one. I can even offer them sound advice on what to wear and what not to wear. All of this has brought me to one conclusion. Things would have been so much better in the garden!

It's Quiet; Too Quiet

Movies today can be extremely graphic, filled with harsh language, sexual situations and, of course, every man's favorite: violence. Things exploding seem to bring joy to men in the same way a shoe sale affects women. Our hearts start pounding, the adrenaline builds and we watch with nervous anticipation to see if the hero of the story, yet again, can survive the horrendous scenarios that they are thrust into.

From these movies, we can glean all kinds of wisdom. From, "Go on without me," to, "It's just a flesh wound," movie dialogue has become a part of our culture. We will quote our favorite lines and re-enact whole scenes that have in some way touched our lives. The movies and television shows we watch shape and mold our character in ways that we cannot begin to fathom. Many of us will come to a point in our lives where we may not remember our children, but we will remember a saying or situation our favorite character said or encountered. For some, it will be,

"Play it again, Sam." Others will hold on to, "May the force be with you." However, I believe the most profound and true-to-life, applicable to child-rearing line ever uttered on stage or screen would have to be, "It's quiet; too quiet."

I have learned through these years at home with my child that if I can't hear her, chances are something is wrong. It may be big, it may be small, but something is going to need fixing or cleaning before the day is done. All quiet times are not bad. There will be rare times-extremely rare between the ages of one and a half and three-where you will fear the worst, only to find that your child is being the perfect angel you knew they were from day one. However, don't let these times fool you. As a rule, if they are quiet, drop whatever you're doing (unless you're holding your other child) and run to whatever room in the house he or she is in. The sooner you find out what they are up to, the better. Why? One reason is because there is less mess to clean up. As they get older and more mobile, the frequency of minor catastrophic events will increase, and you don't want the child hurting themselves. Mostly, though, there's less mess to clean up.

Diapers Should Have Super Glue Tabs!

I'm here to tell you something really important. Poop won't hurt you! It will wash off. One of the worst things you *will* experience—trust me on this—is when you walk into your child's room at naptime. It's one of those quiet moments I mentioned earlier, and you're curious and just a little scared.

This happened to me three times that I remember. It may have happened more, but I have blocked the memory because of its traumatic effect on my life. The worst had to be the first time. After that, I believe she thought my reaction was funny, because my little angel became the Van Gogh of the poop medium.

Unsuspecting, I slowly peeked into my child's room. Her crib was just inside the door and to the right, so when she had fallen asleep, you could typically check on her without disturbing her. As I approached the room, I noticed an odor so I assumed I needed to change her diaper. Imagine my surprise to find a mural. I'm not sure what she was trying to draw, but she had reproduced it on every surface she could reach, including herself, her crib, walls and mattress.

Apparently, she had been studying magic because Houdini would have been proud. There sat my little escape artist, diaper in one hand, nastiness on the other, and a smile that stretched from ear to ear. I'm not going to lie to you. I nearly vomited, but then I remembered rule number one: less to clean up.

I remember crying when I held her for the first time. I remember the joy of her nuzzling against my neck as she slept on my chest. I remember my wife and I being excited when she would have a good "movement." I remember all those things and more, but somehow, at that particular time, I seriously wondered if this were really my child.

I calmly lifted her, touching as little of the child as possible, and set her in the tub. I told her how yucky it was to play in her messy diaper. I pleaded to her sensibilities, explaining how difficult it could be to sleep in a straight jacket. She smiled. I melted. It was then that I realized, "Hey! This isn't that bad. It washes right off with soap and water." I finished cleaning her and then I thought, *If cleaning the walls and her crib are half this easy, I've got it made!*

Of course, my mom was very helpful. She laughed and told me how I had done the same when I was a baby. "Yep, babies do that." The whole time savoring the moment and, I believe, checking off item number 152 on the "When you have a child" list.

My wife was less helpful. She simply said, "You're kidding." Yes, this is like, "Is your refrigerator running?" and, "Do you have *The Cat in the Hat*?" but my favorite prank call of all would have to be anything that starts with, "Guess what your daughter did." Kidding? This was no laughing matter; I had poop on my hands. As I began to cry, she asked me, "Did you clean her up?" I really wanted to say, "No, I thought I'd leave her for you," but I didn't.

After the phone call, I got her dressed and set to the task of cleaning. It wasn't the most pleasant experience, but after twenty minutes of scrubbing, I had her bed back in order and laid her down for her nap. Less than ten minutes later, she fell asleep.

When this happens to you, make sure you wash the child with soap and water and the bed, walls and mattress with Pine-Sol or bleach water, not the other way around. Most importantly, keep your cool. It's not the end of the world; you and your baby are fine. Don't think that you are the only person to go through such a horrid ordeal. Almost every parent I have talked to has told me that their children did the same thing. It doesn't make you a bad parent. What would make you a bad parent is if you didn't bother to clean up after your toddler or infant! You would be a bad parent if you didn't get a little emotional over such an experience. It's natural to be disturbed at the site of your child covered in their own mess. Don't worry! You can make it through this. Compared to dating, this will be a breeze.

Mascara, Scissors and Other Bathroom Messes

A messy diaper isn't the only thing that children will use for making messes. Before my oldest daughter ever learned to open a door or twist off a bottle cap, she mastered the ability to open mascara tubes my wife had thrown away.

We were in the process of potty training, and I was making lunch one day when she had an urge to use the potty. I helped her up on the toilet and then went back to preparing the meal. There she sat, smiling as I told her, "Now you go potty and Daddy will be back in just a minute."

We had been told by several people that one of the best ways to get a child started potty training was to set them on the toilet and periodically check on them to be sure they hadn't fallen in. We would even give her a book and a glass of water to help her relax, but she quickly discovered other activities that made bathroom time much more enjoyable.

I was almost done with lunch, so I asked if she was about done. I walked from the kitchen to the bathroom because things were awfully quiet, and that's when I discovered my daughter had a knack for pen and ink drawing.

Our bathroom is small, so the trash can sits between the tub and the toilet and the toilet sits next to the wall. Typically our bathroom garbage consists of paper products but will occasionally contain an empty make-up container. We'd had no trouble with this setup in the past, so we had little reason to believe it would cause problems in the future, but it did. While I was busily preparing her meal, she had discovered the tube of mascara that my wife had thrown away that morning. I don't exactly understand why. With the complexity of the drawings our daughter had done, the tube had to have been over half full. However, upon later discussion, my wife informed me that it wasn't good any longer because the mascara had begun to clump on the brush. My daughter is decidedly less picky when it comes to clumpy mascara. It worked well for her purposes.

There she was, seated in the exact position as when I had left, but this time, she looked quite different. Her clothes were sitting in front of the toilet, and she had painted her feet, legs and a good portion of her belly with the mascara. When she had run out of room for body painting, she decided that the bathroom would look much better with a painting at sitting level next to the toilet. I never realized how difficult mascara was to remove until I attempted to wash the entire wall and discovered that when it came off, the paint did as well. Then I thought, *Women put this on their eyes?!?*

Of course, I told her that she needed to stay out of the garbage can and she promised that she would, so imagine my surprise when she did the same thing again the next day. Not to the same extent, but she had promised. Then I realized how stupid I was for throwing the thing back into the same garbage can thinking that she wouldn't do it again. As of that point, it became illegal in our house to dispose of anything other than paper in our bathroom garbage can.

The bathroom offers so many opportunities to make a mess, though. I am not a sound sleeper, but often our daughter will wake up and come into the bedroom to get me. On one such morning, she came in, and I noticed she had stuff on her face. We had been having problems with her sneaking candy at night and early in the morning, so I assumed she had found it again. So, at first glance I thought it was candy. Upon closer inspection, I realized it was blood.

No matter how safe you think your house is, or how out of reach you believe something to be for your child, realize that children are curious and they like to explore. I am reminded of the movie *Jurassic Park*, where Doctor Malcolm made the comment, "Nature will find a way." Now, I am not sure if that statement is necessarily true in that context, but it definitely applies to children. They will find a way.

When I saw the mark on her face, I immediately thought the cat had scratched her because she had played too rough with kitty again. I got up to put the cat out on the back porch when I saw a trail of hair. Not a lot, but enough to make me wonder if I was losing mine. I looked in the bathroom and saw that the floor had sprouted tiny hair follicles. We used to keep our hair scissors in a basket on some shelves behind the toilet. There was no way my daughter could reach them without standing on the toilet, but as I said before, children are curious creatures. However, the scissors were neatly back in place, so I assumed my wife had, in some rush, given herself a buzz cut as she often does after again discovering her hair will not do things it doesn't want to or wasn't meant to do.

I turned and looked at my little girl and asked if she had any idea where all the hair had come from. She said, "Yes, Daddy. The man cut my hair like he did Mommy's!" My wife had gone to get a haircut a couple of days before and had taken our daughter with her. She sat and watched as the hairstylist worked his magic and decided, *If he can do that, so can I!* At that moment, I realized her bangs were shorter and a great deal more crooked than I remembered. I also noticed some chunks of hair that were cut off at the scalp. The sides were a little uneven, too. Then I understood. She had gotten up just after her mother had left that morning and decided to give herself a haircut. I have been told that a lot of kids do this. When they do it, it just seems funny. When your own child does this, you realize how easily they can hurt themselves. Needless to say, the scissors are no longer kept in the same place and we had a long talk with her about how dangerous it was to play with anything sharp.

The bathroom horror stories don't end there. Often times she will go potty and come out wrapped in toilet paper or have a train of it trailing off behind her. This is more aggravating than anything else because I can never get it to roll back up right and end up tearing it off and either throwing it away or piling it on top of the roll. I think she even tried fishing once because she said she was done, and I went to do my duty and discovered a line of toilet paper that went from the roll down into the toilet itself.

The most incredible mess of all has to do with her obsession with lotion. Whenever mommy was putting on lotion, our daughter would ask her for some. A little in one hand wouldn't do. She had to have some in both hands. She would vigorously rub it all over herself and her clothes until, finally, with a little help from mom, she had it all rubbed in nice and neat.

One afternoon, when naptime was nearly over, I went in to check on her and noticed that she had fallen asleep with the hair gel bottle in her bed. I thought maybe she had been sleep-styling again, and I walked over to grab the bottle and put it back into the bathroom. I picked it up and, upon further inspection, realized that the bottle was nearly empty. I thought, *My goodness, how much of this does my wife need to get her hair to do what she wants?* That's when I noticed that the bottle was covered in a slimy, sticky substance.

Just so you know, hair gel does *not* have the same effect as a good lotion. It doesn't even have the same effect as a crummy lotion. She had at some point, while I thought she was sleeping, gone into the bathroom and gotten the hair gel and hair spray. She had proceeded to cover herself and her bedding in hair gel. I seriously thought that she was going to stick to the bed, and I would have to take her and her mattress to the car wash to get them separated. After a good bath, for the bed and the child, everything was put back in order.

You will undoubtedly encounter similar situations while raising your children. They can be very stressful. You may even question your sanity! Realize that you probably did something very much like the thing that's got you pulling out your hair by the handful. You see, I believe there is a reason we don't remember much that happens to us before the age of four. It's so our parents can laugh when our children do the same to us. Don't worry - you'll have your turn.

One Thumb or Two

If there is any one thing I believe they should spend additional time on in Lamaze or any other parenting class you might attend, it is what to do when your child reaches the age of toilet training. It is a very trying time, filled with ups, downs and occasional lateral movements that defy reason. Seriously, you will be amazed with the variety of ways children attempt to go potty.

Now, my experience is limited to the realm of girls, and yes, I am quite aware of the rumor going around that boys are easier. To that and to all those who continually offered this little gem when we would approach them looking for advice on the topic, I would have to say, "Just rub it in, why don't you. We have girls and that doesn't help at all!" I couldn't exactly look at the situation at hand with that little tidbit and make it all better! To those of you who said it, I know you meant well, and to those of you who hear it, I feel your pain. After all, you have a job to do, and many parents feel like a colossal failure when they can't communicate this one thought: *When you feel the urge, use the potty, okay, sweetie?*

I am going to let you in on a little secret. Whether your child is a girl or a boy, there is one technique that will work every time. Now, let me clarify this before I go any further. The technique is the same, but the method differs from child to child, and that technique is this: bribery.

Without it, our kids would be in Luvs to this day. We attempted all the traditional methods. Shoot, I even tried giving the kid a book to pass the time; works for me, but none of it helped. We would explain the urge. We would talk about how you need to go right when you feel the urge. We would encourage, saying things like, "You nearly made it that time." We would bash our heads against the wall and scream out to God, "Why am I the worst parent ever; I can't even teach my child to pee in the toilet? Isn't that what makes us civilized? No, I'm a failure. They'll end up on Oprah or Springer, cursing the day they were born, blaming every problem they've had in life on this one simple fact: Mom and Dad never taught me how to use the bathroom, and that's why I'm here today!" We asked friends and family and looked for advice on the internet. All those places had great ideas, but I found our answer (so I thought) in the strangest of places: a television ad.

Those commercials for that particular training pant (you know the ones) the kid comes out of the potty smiling, runs to Mom or Dad while the music fades up and you hear those wonderful words that every parent longs for: "I'm a big kid now." You know the one I'm referring to. I thought, *We gotta have those! Look at the kid; she's smiling, she's a success, she's civilized! She's a big kid now!* So I rushed out and got them, only to discover the magic wasn't in the training pant. Our daughters continued to have a hit or miss average that in baseball would make them all-stars, but in the fast-paced world we live in, was unacceptable to say the least.

Think about all the advice you've gotten. Encourage them. All right, tell that boy or girl they're a big kid when they make it, but what about when they don't? It's always a little awkward. With remorse, we simply say, "That's all right, try harder next time. I know you can do it!" Just a thought, but doesn't that leave the kid wondering, "Am I still big?" And if you say, "You're still my big kid," don't they begin to question our expectations? Maybe this is the makings of a talk show subject. "My parents confused me when I was just a child by encouraging me to use the potty, but they told me I was a big kid no matter what. What do they want from me?"

Seriously, it takes time, patience, encouragement, reward, and–oh–patience. There will be times of success, times of failure and times of success and failure combined. Stop beating yourself up; you are not the major player in this little potty game; you're just the coach. It's not the magic training pants that are the key, it's the attitude we have as parents that can stop the endless leaking (from our eyes, gosh)!

I remember when we first attempted the reward method and we would wonder why our daughter liked spending so much time in the bathroom (see chapter about other bathroom messes). We would probably wonder to this day if I hadn't checked on her once to find her scaling the storage caddy behind the toilet to reach the "reward" box filled with M&M's. You see, on the advice of another, we found this little porcelain/ceramic box thing with a teddy bear that looked like he was standing on a pillow. Inside, we had placed colorful little chocolate buttons that we would award the child when a successful attempt had been logged. They got one for a pee, two for a poop. This method seemed to work for a time; she certainly liked going potty, but when I discovered our little mountain climber, risking her life for a piece of candy-covered chocolate, I began to rethink our approach. I seriously wondered, *What if, when she's a teenager, she has a relapse, forgets what to do and somewhere in the dark recesses of her mind, she recalls a little teddy bear standing on a ceramic pillow and while on a date, maybe the prom, she excuses herself to use the restroom? What if she can't find the little bear hiding the chocolate morsels and she wets herself and runs from the bathroom, crying and screaming, "There's no chocolate; what do I do?"* Talk about an episode of Springer.

I thought about the commercials, the excitement of the children *and* the parents. I began to wonder if maybe it wasn't the magic panties so much as the excitement of success shared by two emotionally connected beings. I thought back to times in my life where I had excelled at something and a parent or other individual who I looked to for direction would reinforce that feeling of excitement I had with genuine excitement of their own for me, and realized that I was on to something.

So I devised a plan, a strategy, if you will, to overcome the problem at hand. First, I identified the problem: wet sheets, couches, carpets, car seats—you get the idea. The goal: using the potty. How to bring those two together? Then it hit me: if I behaved in a certain way towards my child when they produced (so to speak) and they in turn began producing so as to illicit said response, we just might defeat the problem at hand.

I have at times been told how easy it is for me to act like a complete idiot for the benefit of others, and this situation called for just such a performance. And so, every time my daughter would use the bathroom, I would shout, I would dance, and I would give her the thumbs up.

I was the Fonz of the bathroom set. One thumb for pee, two thumbs for poop. It became the natural response to the situation. I even had a chant. I would hear her say, "Daddy, I did it, I did it."

I would ask, "One or two?" She would ball her little fist and lift the appropriate number of digits and we would chant, "One thumb up, one thumb up," or,

"Two thumbs up, two thumbs up," depending upon the results.

My wife got in on the act, as well. I believe the united front from Mom and Dad and the excitement of achievement, of accomplishment, did more to encourage the desired behavior than any piece of chocolate could have possibly done.

Now, our second child required slight modification in approach, but the method remained the same. We basically tricked our children into using the toilet. We bribed them by giving them the excitement in our response that motivated them to be successful so that they could get the response again. Kinda like a rat hitting the feeder button at the end of the maze. Going potty became a conditioned response. Our excitement was heart-felt and no more midnight laundry loads and linen changes was our reward. Hey, when you think about it, who tricked who?

Hey, Bob, What Are You Doing Here?

At almost two, our daughter was obsessed with Veggie Tales. She has all the videos. She has the toys. She sings the songs. I have a Larry-Boy tie and baseball cap, but that's a different story. Anyway, to make a long story short, she loves Bob the Tomato and Larry the Cucumber almost as much as she loves me; sometimes more.

Taking this affection for Veggies into account, I decided that for her second birthday, I would make Bob and Larry cupcakes. I thought, *She is just gonna love this!* I had no idea what would happen, but I knew that this would be the best birthday she had ever had, all because of these cupcakes with green and red frosting.

I got my cake mix and stayed up late into the night the day before the festivities. I bought vanilla frosting and used red and green food coloring to frost the cupcakes. I got white and black gel to do the eyes and I made noses out of Skittles. They were so cool.

Of course, the first couple birthdays and Christmases are more exciting to the parents than the child, but I didn't care. She was going to have the perfect birthday celebration.

We took her to her favorite pizza place, and she loved it. The food, the presents, the attention, what more could a child ask for? Then, it was time. Let me advise you, think twice before you make your two-year-old child something to eat that looks like her most favorite thing in the world. We sang "Happy Birthday," then passed out the cupcakes.

Everyone at our table got very quiet as my little girl admired this work of art her daddy had prepared for her. She then cocked her head to the side, looked at the cupcake and asked, "Hey, Bob, what are you doing here?" After we had a good laugh, I peeled the paper off my Larry cupcake and began to dig in. I looked at her and asked, "Honey, aren't you going to eat your cupcake?"

You would have thought I had dragged Barney into the street and began wailing on him. She started to get upset because I wanted her to eat her hero. She even cried a little bit, and I felt like the biggest moron on the planet.

Faith in God and the Power of Veggie Tales

I have a name for large purple dinosaurs: Gigantus Annoyasaurus. Don't get me wrong, my girls love the big guy, but there are just some things about him that I don't get. First of all, dinosaurs are extinct. Second, he's just so creepy. Third, it makes no sense. I mean, a stuffed animal coming to life and taking children on exciting adventures? My kids are scared of dinosaurs.

There was a time in our home when the "B" word (No, stick with me: B-A-R-N-E-Y) was off-limits. He wasn't spoken of. It was as though saying his name might cause him to jump from the television into our living room. Trust me, he may be a dinosaur, but I would have beaten him into a pile of quivering purple goo.

It's not fair, really. He never did anything to me; I just can't stand him. Even now, those songs echo in the dark corners of my mind; it's horrifying! I don't know what we would have done if we hadn't been introduced to a singing cucumber and his friend, the tomato, by a family member. They were the perfect alternative to Mr. Annoyasaurus. At that particular time in life, we lived in a house smaller than many apartments, and we had one television. Whatever was on, everybody watched. Believe me, I thanked God for veggies that sing and dance while cracking jokes. My kids only understood occasionally, but I got every one.

Now some may think that to be selfish, but I don't. Some may think it childish, but not me. Some may find it downright ridiculous, but during the times we shared watching Larry-Boy with his super-suction ears or when we watched as Junior overcame his fear of monsters, opportunities to talk about faith as a family inevitably arose.

Now before you say, "Hey, too much television will rot your mind," let me say, I agree. People in America today are so driven to be entertained that the days of going into the woods with a stick pretending to be a great explorer searching for a lost world are gone. (Trust me, it was lots of fun.) Kids need to be encouraged to go outside and play. They need to be inspired to be creative. And while most things on television aren't worth the time spent watching, God has provided a number of alternatives that don't fall into the typical "Christian" genre (a lot of which isn't worth watching, either).

Songs like "God is Bigger" helped my girls through times when they were scared of the dark, or when the thunder of an approaching storm was so loud it shook the house.

I remember one time when there was a tornado warning in the middle of the night at our little house without a basement and no central room. We huddled together under a comforter in one of the safest places in the house where three doorways formed the tiniest of hallways, singing and talking about God being bigger and how there was nothing to be afraid of because he would protect us.

Thank you, Big Idea, for giving parents a choice that is relevant and is a quality product. There are others out there trying to do the same thing, and I appreciate your efforts, too, but for some reason, a cucumber singing about his missing hairbrush just appeals to us.

The Wisdom of a Child

Some of the most interesting things I know, I learned from my daughters. From the first moment they were able to speak, they began to share bits of wisdom that I haven't been able to find from any other source.

Things like, "Daddy, you can't go potty with your pants on!" What a great piece of information. And really, who else would care enough to share such knowledge. Most people would just let you pee your pants.

I think this gift comes from their mother, who has often shared things with me that, though occasionally confusing, are no less valuable. I remember a time before the children when she informed me that, if we didn't open the windows, the curtains were going to die. Not quite on the level of Confucius (have you ever noticed how close that is to "confusion"?) but wise none the less. (She meant to say, "If we don't open the curtains, the plants are gonna die," but that wouldn't have made nearly as huge of an impact on me as what she did say!).

Some of their less endearing traits, they have learned from me. For example, when we are driving, you will often hear from the back seat, "Daddy, these cars are driving me crazy." They learned that from me. Driving can be very challenging, not because I lack the ability, but because it seems like whenever any one else gets behind the wheel, they do! That being said, this is a valuable lesson best learned before you make a similar mistake.

Your children will be very free with information. They will be glad to tell other people just what you think of them. Smash your finger with a hammer and slip up, cursing the hammer's very existence, don't worry about confession. If they heard it, they'll confess it for you.

And that isn't limited to things they hear. It extends to things they see. I realized this was a problem when a gentleman I respected in the church informed me that we might want to shut our bedroom door even if we think they're sleeping. Remember, they hear and see (and share) everything!

Many of our celebrations and family's excursions have included an interesting bit of information that, if not for my children, I would never have known. Sometimes just driving down the road gives opportunity to learn just how wise they are. Once, while driving, our oldest daughter told my wife, "You know, some people see red as green." Her mother asked,

"What are you talking about, child?" She simply replied, "Sometimes when it is red, they go."

Their wisdom isn't limited to the everyday. They have a spiritual knowledge that's origin escapes me, but it makes sense. Things like, "I've got to hold on tight because I don't want my balloon to float all the way up to Jesus," or on one exchange where our youngest informed us she wanted to give the moon a hug. When she was told it was to far away, she simply said, "Well then God needs to pick me up so I can give it a hug!"

With all they seem to know, there are still some things they don't quite get. Like the idea that when they talk to you over the phone, you can see what they are looking at, or if you grab a balloon filled with helium, you'll be able to fly around the house. (I don't think she really believed this one. I think she wanted to see her sister try it and fall down so she could laugh!) Sometimes they'll think your eyebrows are made from chocolate and think that pennies are food, but it will pass. (Literally!)

Don't worry! Even though they possess this wisdom, you are still needed. They need your direction. Yes, for many of us, they are smarter, but they don't know that! So take heart and read some more; it makes us look smart!

I Will Sing a New Song to the Lord.

Not all the things my kids have taught me are silly. One of the most revealing spiritual lessons I have gotten came from the heart of a child.

In the book of Psalms, the Bible tells us through the writing of King David to, "sing a new song to You, oh God." (Psalms 144:9, NIV) I never quite understood the true meaning of that particular scripture until my oldest daughter showed me. In truth, this one event illustrated a number of verses more vividly than any Bible study could begin to explain.

We were visiting her grandparents on a Saturday in March. On our way home from dinner, she began singing a song that she had made up, totally heart-felt worship from the heart of a four-year-old. I sat there awestruck to hear my child singing about how much she loved Jesus and that one day she would get to see him and hug him and be with him. No false motives, no fear of what others may think, just pure worship. This was a child of God singing a love song to her LORD.

It was awesome to sit there and listen to this song that she came up with. It opened my eyes to the true meaning of Psalm 96:1: "Sing to the LORD a new song; sing to the LORD, all the earth." (NIV)

I could picture God in heaven, smiling. I wonder if there was celebrating in the streets. Did Jesus weep for joy over the love and faith of this little child?

A few weeks later we were at a concert where the band Mercy Me sang her favorite song, "I Can Only Imagine." I stood on the hillside and absorbed the awesome experience of people worshipping and praising God.

I have had a chance to sing with our girls in church. I have watched them worship. I have seen them share a song in a chapel service. No matter where they are at or who they are in front of, my children will share the love they have for God in their hearts.

I wish that I had that faith. Even as a youth minister, there are times when I hold back or I think about who might be listening besides the LORD, and I have been completely ashamed. There is something to the whole idea of having faith as a child.

My children will believe in something that they cannot see or understand simply because I tell them it is so. They have no doubts that when they praise God, he hears them. I have doubted because of my own lack of faith when I, at times, have taken my eyes off of him and began to focus on the storm that's raging around me. Life happens. There is nothing that I can do to change the past; all I can do is look to the future and believe that God will do what he has promised. It's easier for a child to understand this because they don't try to overcomplicate things.

Children take the Bible and what it says as a simple statement that God loves us. Adults try to explain the Word in ways that we can easier relate to. Children just accept it as truth; we have to know why it's truth and who it's true to. That's why it is so important to "train a child in the way they should go" (Proverbs 22:6, NIV) when they are young.

Both of my girls have accepted Christ as Savior. We continue instructing them so that, one day, when they begin to have questions of their own they will have a firm foundation to fall back on. I don't have all the answers, but I know where to look for direction. If I can teach my children that simple truth, that direction comes from God, then I will know that they will never be lost. The Bible says it; I have to believe it.

I encourage my children to sing about God. I want them to express the way they feel about him. I sing with them when I know the words and when I don't, I just listen and smile. Their faith is a source of strength for me and has helped me through times of uncertainty. So we sing a new song whenever we can and when we don't have a new song, the older ones work well, too!

Prayer Time

One of the most touching experiences I have ever had was hearing my daughter pray for me when I wasn't feeling well. It wasn't some long, drawn-out thing. We sat down for dinner and she asked to say the blessing.

"Dear Jesus," she said. "Thank you for this day and bless this food. Touch Daddy and make him feel better. Touch Mommy and keep her safe. In Jesus' name, amen."

Nothing scripted. A very simple prayer that was as effective as any prayer I've ever heard. That got me to thinking how sweet the sound of a child's prayer must be to God. I can picture him sitting in heaven with a grin from ear to ear. She wasn't prompted; she just presented what was on her heart to him, and he listened. I did feel better.

I want to encourage you to urge your children to pray. As parents, we often try to force our children to do things the way we want them to. At bedtime, my wife and I would take turns sitting with her and reminding her to pray for this person and that, determining who she should pray for and when she was done. The LORD began to work on me about this and made me realize that she was praying my prayer for her rather what she wanted to pray about. This may seem silly to some of you, but think about how you would feel if someone sat beside you as you prayed and told you who and what to pray about.

Eventually, prayer time became more of a routine and a pattern. Prayer should be a habit, but it should never be something that we just spout off without meaning or feeling in the words we speak. At bedtime, she had a list of things she prayed for and, if she missed one or she said them in the incorrect order, she would start over. I had to teach her to pray without influencing the things she prayed about. It's harder than it sounds. If she wants to pray for her hair, I guess that's okay, even though it doesn't make sense to me. If she forgot to pray for her hair, she got frustrated with herself. She would start over from the beginning, praying for her hair in the proper place. I would encourage her, reminding her that she doesn't have to pray exactly the same way every time. I would share with her that sometimes, the Holy Spirit would bring things to your attention that you needed to pray for at that moment and that sometimes, things aren't necessarily as important as we think they are. That doesn't mean that God doesn't care about those things; it means that from time to time, our focus is shifted from one thing to another, all very difficult to explain to a child.

We started small. We talked about prayer in the Bible, and we looked at how Jesus prayed. I would pray, and then I would encourage my girls to pray for what was on their hearts. I didn't do this to influence what they were praying for so much as to help them see that we can talk to God just like he is sitting right next to us while we talk, because he is.

When things would happen or people were sick, we prayed. We took turns praying for the meal and, slowly, we got away from those cute rhyming prayers that are fine to teach beginning prayer but don't say a whole lot that is truly heart-felt.

I remember being shocked at how much my oldest daughter was impacted by the death of my grandfather. She had hardly known him, but his passing caused her grief for over a year after his death. I would find myself missing him, but it was as though it had just happened for my daughter.

I thought about it and I realized that I had not lost anyone as a child. The first death that touched my life closely didn't happen until I was nearly a teenager, and I understood a little better life and death. At three years old, my daughter didn't have that understanding; she just knew that her great-grandpa was gone. So we prayed, and we talked, then we prayed some more, and we got through it. He is still missed. It was her first experience with the grief loss causes. When she mentions it now, we know how to deal with it.

We pray and there is more power in that than you can imagine. Teach your children to pray and let them hear you praying. It will help build their faith and it will give you a firm foundation to build your relationship as parent and child. You can never go wrong with prayer.

Our Newest Arrival and Assisted Living

When our second child was born, I had no idea the vast wealth of parenting expertise our firstborn would have to offer. She has seemed to have more knowledge of what is good for a child and how that child should be raised than we have. She has been extremely free with her advice. She has even decided to enact her parenting strategies without first consulting us. Once again, this was something not covered in our prenatal parenting classes.

In my mind, I would picture her rushing into the room to help her little sister only to end up dragging her through the house by her leg or that she would pick her up by the waist but upside down so that her head was bouncing off the ground. I would have nightmares that they would wake up before me and she would decide to help sissy from her crib. I remember being terrified that our oldest would try to change her sister's diaper or that she would decide to be the world's youngest hair stylist and give the baby a hair cut. Can you say trauma ward? I even remember thinking, *What if they wake up and she decides to give her baby sister a bath?* None of those things happened, but I worried about them for months following the birth.

I eventually began to welcome some of the help. Raising two children, one a toddler and one an infant, is a challenging prospect. I came to a point where I would have been overjoyed if she had taken it upon herself to change a diaper, but it never happened. In fact, during those first few years, the more I welcomed her help with her sister, the less she was willing to do. Once the new baby smell wore off, she began looking for new ways to amuse herself. It was as if she became bored with the idea.

I know some of it had to do with the demands a baby placed on my attention. So, I tried to involve her as much as possible in the process. This had mixed results. Sometimes I would praise her for the job she did. Other times, I would have to scold her. She was always closely supervised, and I do believe it was the right choice to allow her to be a part of the process, but there were times when I found myself wishing for a quiet corner somewhere in a room with soft padded walls and no windows. I would say things like, "Don't pull on her arms like that," or, "She has no teeth, she can't chew steak! Get that out of her mouth!" Well, that second one was a bit of an exaggeration, but you get the idea.

To a child, a baby is like a new plaything. Once the

packaging comes off and the excitement of the first couple of playtimes passes, it's just one more thing to destroy. Think about it. You spend twenty dollars on a doll that ends up sitting in a toy box, contorted in positions the manufacturer never intended the doll to bend into. It was the most incredible toy the day they got it, and now its old news. Better things have come along to take the place of that once loved toy that's now missing half its hair and part of a leg. That new baby was exciting, but now it's taking away from Mom and Dad's time with me and it smells.

Think like a child for a moment. Would you still want that baby, or would you just stick it in the bottom of the box, hoping maybe it might just be forgotten so that the next best thing to come along can take its place?

It drove me crazy at first, and it still irritates me from time to time. As they have grown older, the mothering tendencies of the oldest have only increased, but I understand it. It's a hierarchy. The oldest has more seniority and, as such, has been through these things before. She is older and wiser and has something that she believes to be of value to offer the younger. We have all been there. We have all wanted to feel like we had something important to give. It makes us feel needed, and that is something we all long to feel: necessary.

Of course, it has to be dealt with. We are the parents, and we are prepared, hopefully, for the challenges that come with that authority. Sibling rivalry is worsened if there isn't some kind of balance established. Boundaries need to be set, or hurt feelings will result.

In the end, our oldest never did drag her sister through the house by her leg. She did pick her up a couple of times, and I recall her pulling her from the couch a time or two, but if she were allowed to continue bossing her sister around simply because she is the oldest, she may as well have drug her from one end of the house to the other, banging her head on every step and door frame along the way. She can help, and she does, and when it's left to that, everything works well, but when she decides to be the mom, that's when things get broken.

Sibling Rivalry

One area I was completely unprepared for was the area of sibling rivalry. I was an only child until I turned eleven. I had no idea how vicious the fighting between your kids can be. They will lie and cheat. They will fight verbally and physically. It's like politics without the interns and scandal.

There are days when it seems like I am more of a referee than a parent. Having girls, it's worse because everything is a crisis. I tell them I love them every day, and yet they compete to win our affection. They jockey for position like racers at a starting gate. They will trample anything or anyone who gets in their way. It's madness!

I have watched as my two little angels have crawled over each other to be the first to complete a task I have given them. If I ask one of them to do something, they both try to be the first to get it done. The youngest is especially prone to this jealous behavior.

I think sometimes she is jealous of her big sister

just because she is bigger. I remember wanting to be older so that I could do more things. No matter how much I stress that she is special for who she is, there is always this underlying tension that, sometimes, comes roaring to the surface.

Even as I write this, the not-so-subtle tones of disharmony ring throughout the halls of our happy home. Even now, as the little vein every parent seems to have throbs as once again you explain to the children how hitting, biting, scratching, yelling, physical or verbal abuse of any kind will not be tolerated, I am reminded of what a blessing it is to be a parent. Really, if it weren't for us, who knows what the little savages, I mean, darlings, would become.

It seems so odd to me that two loving children can go from hugging to fighting in less time than it takes to break an egg. The drama is never ending and usually is the result of some complete misunderstanding. They haven't even begun dating yet. LORD, help me when that day comes! I have often wished for a supernatural intervention in which God would make it impossible for the two to argue. As yet, that has not come to pass.

Nothing brings me closer to tears and a straight jacket than the sounds of my girls mercilessly beating each other because they can't find their hair bow or one touched something that belonged to the other. I have found a remedy that seems to bring an immediate end to the hostilities. I wonder if it would work in the world of international diplomacy.

I look them square in the eye, and I simply say, "Okay, now fight to the death." The first time they were completely shocked; now they just look at me and each other and they laugh, and then we resolve the situation accordingly. I would love to have one of those bouncy boxing rings with the oversized gloves and protective head gear or two of those gigantic sumo suits that I could put on them when the need arises and allow them to beat each other senseless in relative safety. For now, just the thought of fighting to the death makes them see the silliness of the fight in the first place. Thankfully, they didn't take me up on it the first time I said it.

Use this technique with caution. It may not work for your children. I know my kids well enough that I realized they would laugh and we would be able to get to the bottom of the situation. Of course, they both have to sit as close to me as possible. And what's it mean when neither will stop hugging me until the other lets go first?

Road Trips and Rest Stops

If scientists would investigate, I believe they would discover a direct correlation between senility and the number of road trips you take with your kids. The effect is increased exponentially if you have a child with a thirst bigger than their bladder.

When I was younger, my grandparents took me on a trip across country from Michigan to Texas. I remember the trip fondly, and I believe I developed my own road trip strategy from watching my grandfather as he drove across the plains and through the mountains. The van was fully loaded with drinks and lunch meat. My grandmother would make lunch as we rolled down the road in that comfortable Ford van. Not a minivan, it was a full-sized van with captain's chairs and bench seats. It spoke something to me and that was, "The less you stop, the quicker you get to where you're going."

It also showed me the best situation for traveling with children. I would frequently request that my grandfather stop so I could use the rest room and he would laugh (his laugh was unique, and I still smile when I think of it). He would say, "Well, Tob, we just stopped twenty miles back! Why didn't you go then?" It was a simple question, and I had the answer. I would look at him and say, "I didn't have to go then." We stopped at almost every road side attraction we passed that was within twenty minutes of the highway, and I still felt it necessary to inspect every rest stop from Jackson, Michigan, to El Paso, Texas. "Why didn't you go then?" I didn't realize it at the time, but those words would come back to haunt me as I traveled with my own kids. I think it's all because of the curse.

You know the one: "Someday, when you grow up and have kids of your own, I hope you have one that acts just like you. Then you'll understand what I mean!" Truer words were never spoken. I have two girls who act very much like me, and now I understand so much more than my parents and grandparents ever tried to tell me. I have said the exact words of my grandfather on a number of road trips and, completely exasperated, heard an eerily similar response: "I didn't have to," or "I tried, but I didn't go," and worst of all, "I did, but I gotta go again."

How is it possible that a little girl would have to go potty twice within the space of fifteen minutes? I sniffed what was in her sippy cup. I know it wasn't coffee! I think there is nothing that can drive a man to the brink of a psychotic break quicker than having

400 miles to go and stopping twice within a ten-mile stretch of road.

Those trips are killers—the ones where an eight-hour drive takes eleven. Sometimes it is unavoidable because of work schedules or school and I have to drive during the day when the cursed sunlight draws the attention of a little child to everything and everyone you pass. Whenever possible, I drive at night.

It's great! Almost like a vacation within a vacation. The wife and kids are sleeping, and I drive across the peaceful countryside making great time, chewing on sunflower seeds (they'll keep you awake, believe me) and listening to late night talk radio (they'll keep you awake, believe me). Talk about your entertainment! Occasionally, the solitude is disrupted by the cry of a child or my wife, but generally, the trip can be made with minimal interruption and, as every man knows, it's always a race. "Can I shave off ten minutes?" If I can keep them asleep for the entire trip, you better believe it!

Avoid stopping for gas, even if the price is phenomenal. Trust me, if you stop, you will pay more in the long run. The extra bathroom breaks alone will kill your gas mileage. Not to mention, "Can I have this or that?" Then you think, *I could go for a bite myself*, which ends up causing you to be sleepy (avoid turkey sandwiches while driving, not a good mix). It all leads to more delays and you have a schedule to keep and a new best time to set, remember? By the time you buy all the snacks, drinks, and extras that they just had to have, you could have paid an extra dollar per gallon and still come out ahead. Don't stop, just drive!

If you must drive in the daytime, let me suggest an investment that has brought me out of the dark and into the light. Kids will ride for hours while watching their favorite shows and never have to pee. It's like the little image on the portable DVD gives them the bladder of a camel. They won't eat; they won't drink... if they have headphones, they don't even talk! Now that's worth the fifty bucks right there. Give your wife a new book before you start the trip, and you're golden.

So sit back, set the cruise control and slip into that place where you're at your best, behind the wheel of an automobile. Just don't stop and ask for directions—what kind of man are you?

Wasted Days and Sleepless Night After Night . . .

(The Calendar Means Nothing)

Sleep is for sissies. Who needs it anyway? Actually, our kids didn't do too bad sleeping through the night. They might have woken up once or twice, typically to be fed, and then they would usually go right back to sleep. For those of you who have problems in this area, my only suggestion is to wear them out while they are awake. Have a baby Olympics or something. Maybe even cut naptime short; if that doesn't work I don't know what to tell you. I guess we were just blessed with perfect kids most nights.

Then there were the nights when our girls were sick. There were times when the weather was raging, and they were scared. My favorite of all would have to be those times when they just didn't want to go to bed. Our oldest fought sleep horribly. Once she was asleep, she was great, but getting her there was a challenge. We would rock her to sleep and the instant her body touched the crib mattress, she was screaming as though someone had just beheaded her teddy bear. I even considered becoming her mattress, because if I laid her on my chest while I lay on the couch, she would sleep for hours, but I was always afraid I might squish her. So I might have dozed off, but it wasn't always restful.

Our youngest child takes after her mother—if there is a place to lay your head, she can fall asleep. Our oldest takes after me. I don't like to sleep. I guess I am afraid I might miss something, but I like having the option if I am tired. The fighting sleep game got old. At first, we would put her in her crib and check on her if she cried. Big mistake. We eventually got to a point where we would leave her and listen for the type of crying. Our neighbors would be over playing a game, and they would ask us, "Are you going to get her?" We would explain that she was fine, and she would eventually fall asleep. Sometimes we would pick her up, but more often than not, she just needed to be alone.

Those times passed. She eventually got to a point where she would reluctantly lay down without crying and drift off. Sometimes it took five minutes, sometimes she would still be awake an hour later, but she stopped crying and fighting it, and that was great for us.

Sickness was the worst. They would wake up in the middle of the night; sometimes they had thrown up, sometimes they hadn't, but there was a good chance they would before they made it to the toilet. It doesn't happen as much now, but there are still the occasional nights where I find myself cleaning a mattress at 3:00 am.

I'm not sure which is worse: the night vomits or the coughing fits that last forever! I am certain that neither of them is pleasant for the child or the parent. Who wants to spend the evening cleaning up after someone or trying to sooth them? I guess doctors or nurses, but I'm not one of those! When I wake up, I want to stay up, no matter if I have been sleeping for an hour or a full night. There is nothing that makes a parent feel more helpless than watching as their child is sick and knowing there is nothing you can do for them. You wish you could take that cold upon yourself, but you know that you can't, so you sit by and do what you can. You sing to them. You hold them. You clean their messes, hoping and praying that God will touch them and help them feel better.

I admire parents whose children have terminal illness, and I feel for them. I cannot begin to understand how they must be feeling. I know from my own experiences that they have to feel helpless. Somehow, most of them find the strength to do what they need to for their child's sake, and that is impressive.

Night is not the only time when challenges come up. It's as if the children have no concern whether I stick to my schedule or not. They seem to think that the calendar means nothing! A child doesn't care if they have an appointment in fifteen minutes, and the office is twenty minutes away. They drag their feet and pull on their coats as though they had all the time in the world. All the while, Mom or Dad is wearing out their cell phone pushing the little button to turn on the backlight so they can see what time it is now. It's like they don't care if they get where they have to be on time, and it drives me crazy!

Don't despair. There are some simple changes you make to your own schedule to cope for those instances when you have been awake for twelve hours and still have accomplished nothing.

First, develop the ability to lie to your children. Now, I'm not talking about big lies that matter, I'm talking about setting all the clocks in the house ahead and not telling them. I'm talking about writing down appointment times a half hour early so that you can be there on time. I am even condoning not telling your children everything you have to do while highlighting those things that might appeal to their sense of urgency. It's not really lying, it's manipulating, and they do it to you.

Second, do everything you can to make your children take a nap until they are teenagers. Once they become teenagers, all they want to do is sleep and eat, so getting them to take a nap is less challenging. Getting a nine-year-old to lie down after getting off the bus from school takes a miracle! Think of what you might be able to accomplish with that extra half an hour.

Lastly, try to do those things that are really important before your children are awake or while they are at school. They can't mess up your schedule if you don't give them the chance. While the calendar is important for them when it affects them, it doesn't mean as much when they feel that the activity has nothing to do with them, so combine events for maximum participation. If you want this or you would like to go here, then we must accomplish this by a certain time. It works no matter how small or trivial the thing they want is to you, because it's important to them and at some point, most children go through a phase where their wants and desires are all that matter. Don't worry, when they turn thirty, you'll be able to relate to them again!

And Yes, They Are Angels

(but only when they are sleeping)

I would like to pose a simple question. How is it that a child can be starving to death one minute and then when you have placed a perfectly acceptable meal in front of them, they are full or they don't feel good? A child who would normally be considered perfect and well-behaved can become a juvenile delinquent in the time it takes to turn your head to glance at the clock.

If you don't believe it, leave your finicky child alone one night at the dinner table with a plate full of vegetables. See how quickly they look for anyone watching and then, when the coast is clear, they sneak to the trash can and dispose of the evidence. Dogs are also a means of disposal, but kids will typically use the most efficient method to get to what they really want to be doing. I have found forks, spoons and on one occasion, a plate still containing the evidence on it placed in the trash. When confronted about it, I was smiled at to see if I thought it was as funny as my child did. When it became obvious that I didn't find it humorous, the look changed instantly from smile to a pouting, apologetic, foot-shuffling "I'm sorry," with an accompanying, "I won't do it again, I promise!" And she didn't ever throw the plate away again, she just scraped the vegetables or whatever food item was keeping her from her desired task before exclaiming, "I'm finished."

She was finished all right! Kids will test you in every situation and circumstance. They will stretch you and twist you around until you become a human pretzel. You did it, too, remember! They are angels; way deep down inside of every child, there is a sweet side that isn't always motivated by personal gain. It isn't always evident and sometimes you have to really look for that side, but it's there, and not just when they're sleeping.

The same child who has, on a number of occasions, excused herself from the dinner table through creative means has hugged me and told me she loves me for no reason. When I have felt ill, she has tried to take care of me to the best of her ability. She has made her bed or picked up her room for nothing more than my approval and the knowledge that I am proud of her.

At the same time, she has lied about silly things, not because she was trying to frame her sister in some elaborate plot, but because she is a child. Children make mistakes, and they need a mom and a dad who love them enough to correct them. There isn't a magical formula that, when applied to a child, will guarantee instant results. Each child is different, and what works for one won't always work for their siblings. Trial and error is necessary, and where one child will respond to a stern rebuke, a sibling may require additional correction. That correction can be any number of things, but isn't limited to a spanking. You have to be creative with discipline while at the same time remembering that the Bible gives clear instruction that sometimes a child needs to be corrected with more than just words or a timeout.

There are certain things that a child is and things a child is not. Children are not stupid. They know their parent should be correcting them for mistakes they make. We are charged with instructing our children in "the way they should go." When that is lacking, a child will do what anyone will do in a situation where leadership is lacking: they will assert themselves and take on roles they are not prepared for. A child doesn't necessarily long for correction, but when given correctly, there is a part of them that receives it as love.

Constantly repeating to my children, "Pick up your toys or I'll throw them away," probably won't bring about the desired result. However, when I sit with them and explain how I expect things to be and then I show them what I desire, they are much more accommodating. When I accompany this with praise for good behavior or discipline for poor behavior, then I am truly instructing them.

There will be times when your child doesn't finish their meatloaf because they don't like it even though it was their favorite the day before. They will leave dirty socks in the corners of their room and tell you that they don't know how they got there. Yes, your child will at some point even look at you with the most pitiful look on their face and swear to you that they didn't do the very thing that you just saw them doing, and that's okay. It isn't a personal attack against you, and it doesn't make you a failure as a parent. It's at times like these where trust is born.

A child wants to know that, even though they are imperfect and they make mistakes, you will love them unconditionally. In a strange way, correction increases trust between a parent and child. So love them enough to correct them.

Within Limits

The ability of a child to stretch the limits or boundaries that you set for them is astounding. In all sports, there are individuals who test the limits of human capability. They amaze us with their athletic prowess and seemingly super-human skill. Then there are those who are great, but are not quite at that level. They have the skills through hard work and perseverance. Then there are some who are known for their willingness to bend the rules to their advantage. They whine about every call that goes against them, and sometimes that whining pays off. Maybe they intimidate the official or maybe the official is just sick of hearing them complain. Either way, they are known for their complaints just as much as they are known for their skill. This last group is the best example of what it can be like to deal with children.

As a parent, I have discovered that children will do just about anything to get what they want when they want it. Good children will manipulate you to achieve their desired outcome. They will push your limits and test your patience to the point that you understand why your father had no hair and your mother went prematurely grey. They are like those athletes who complain no matter how obvious the infraction. They want the boundaries to apply for everyone else, but when they are applied to them, they want some flexibility.

I believe as parents, we have to establish boundaries for our children from an early age and that we have to stick to them. There can be some flex, a little give and take, but for the most part, we should stick to our guns so we don't send mixed signals to our kids. That being said, when your child looks at you with those puppy dog eyes and asks "please" and says "I love you," it can be very easy to give in.

Your children will find a way around your limits. They will swear ignorance of the rules or temporary memory lapse to avoid the penalty for going out of bounds. Each of us has our breaking point, so it is important for you to know how far is too far for your kids to push you; otherwise, you may end up as a story on the six o'clock news.

I always set the boundaries shorter than I am willing to let them go. I know they will try to push and stretch past the lines I have set, so I set them a little shorter so that there is a little cushion.

When I was growing up, my parents would jokingly tell me to go play in traffic (I hope it's a joke; otherwise, that's just sick!) I don't believe they truly wanted me to go play in traffic, but it's great for this purpose. Say my kids asked me, "Dad, can we go play in traffic?" I am not going to allow them to play in traffic no matter how much they beg and plead with me. This is a set limit, and there is no flexing in this line. I will not allow my girls to play in traffic and that's that. However, that doesn't mean I won't let them go outside at all. That would just be cruel. In the same way, I wouldn't let my kids play with matches. It doesn't mean they can't look at fire. It does mean I don't want them creating it easily. If my kids are going to make fire, they need to impress me by rubbing two sticks together or by using a piece of chocolate and a soda can. My kids know that these are boundaries that, if they cross them, there are stiff penalties that result.

They also know that they aren't supposed to get a soda from the refrigerator without asking. Somehow this has not been as firmly set in stone. They know that candy is not to be taken into the playroom, and that they can't have chocolate without asking. Yet, time and again when we do a good cleaning, I find wrappers mixed in with their toys. I think they get this from their mom, who frequently hides her candy habit from me, but I know she's got a problem.

"Ask before you have" is no less a rule than "don't play with matches or car bumpers" (especially while the vehicle is moving); but, they seem to be interpreted differently. Maybe I unconsciously put more emphasis on one set of boundaries than the other, or maybe it's a matter of threat level. Let's face it. The consequences of playing in traffic may be much more severe than those of eating chocolate in the playroom. Chocolate in small doses is typically harmless; car bumpers or roaring fires are dangerous in any amount.

Some children will push every boundary set for them. Some will pick and choose. All kids will test the limits of your patience and your will. It's a natural part of growing up and becoming independent. You are still in charge and our kids aren't the only ones who need boundaries. I have to know how far is too far so that I know when to step back and take a moment to regain my composure. Count to ten, say "woosaw," or whatever you do to gain control. You will lose your patience, and that's okay. What's not okay is crossing your own boundaries. Those lines should never be crossed.

Crime & Punishment

Probably the single most difficult part of parenting is disciplining your child. You will question yourself, your sanity and your child's hearing. Trust me, there will be days where the little cartoon of the frazzled lady, her hair standing on end, ragged smile and the words, "I've got one nerve left, and you're getting on it," will make perfect sense. Children will test your patience, your nerve, and your will. But it's all right; we're bigger than them. Besides, we know how to get to McDonalds, and they don't.

First of all, there are things my parents said to me that I promised myself I would never say to my kids, but guess what? I lied. I don't recall ever saying the biggie. You know the one. "I just want you to know, this is going to hurt me worse than it hurts you!" I used to think that that was quite possibly the dumbest thing ever said by anyone, but now I understand it.

A child is an extension of ourselves. We see them as we hope they will be: perfect. Kids aren't the only ones who put someone on a pedestal. Every time they fail, we see it as a failure in our abilities to parent. Each time we punish a child, we feel as though it is a small reflection of our own frailties. We magnify our problems and then we magnify theirs.

If a child is a little rambunctious, today we take them to see a doctor. I remember if I had ever, I don't know, been in the bathroom playing in the water and turning a light off and on, my parents didn't take me to see a psychologist, they pulled me aside and expressed their dislike of the behavior I was displaying. My grandparents did it, too. If I acted up at school, my principal would adjust my attitude-sometimes a little, sometimes a lot. He didn't immediately call my mom and say, "This child is just too unruly, get him some drugs, will you!"

I'm not saying that there aren't legitimate circumstances for children needing psychiatric treatment; there are. But many times, what's needed is strict discipline from an authority figure, not just from a parent. Many parents today weren't disciplined as a child, so they have no idea what to do when their own child breaks the rules. Time-outs don't always work. Sometimes you have to get your hands dirty. It doesn't always involve corporal punishment. It takes a parent getting involved.

To borrow a quote from the Bible, "If you do not punish your children, you don't love them, but if you love your children, you will correct them." (Proverbs 13:24, NCV) There are times where a spanking might be necessary. There have been many times I have walked through a store and considered asking a mother who was being completely disrespected by her child if she would like me to assist her. I might even offer her my belt. But physical punishment is ineffective if the child doesn't believe the parent loves them or cares about them.

Involvement and love are the two greatest deterrents to having a rebellious child. Now I know that throughout this book I have stressed the importance of showing your children love. Sometimes loving someone means correcting them. Too many parents are allowing television and schools to raise their children and leaving the discipline behind for a quick visit to the psychologist, or to a doctor, where they leave the child and wait for the professional to come back with their opinion.

Parenting isn't a part-time job or responsibility. It isn't only something we do when our children make us proud or when it's convenient. It's a full-time, 24/7 commitment to be there, no matter the situation.

For single parents, this is an overwhelming concept. They have their plate filled with providing everything for the household. Discipline isn't always high on the priority list. More often than not, keeping some sort of order is. The high rate of divorce in this country has lead to an overly-medicated generation of children who have no idea what true discipline is; they think it comes from a pill.

A child isn't a bandage for a bad relationship. Typically a child will only add more stress to an unstable marriage rather than solidify it. Raising a child well in this time is a difficult proposition, but it can be done.

Believe me, it will hurt you more than it hurts the child. There have been many times where, while playing, I have swatted one of my girls on the butt far harder than I had intended, and way harder than I have when I was correcting them. When it's playfully done, a spanking brings laughter; when it's given out of correction, it leads to tears. Why?

The emotional connection of parents who are involved with their child's life is the key to disciplining effectively. I have two daughters. For one, my being disappointed in her behavior is as effective as a spanking. For the other, sometimes a spanking is necessary. However, whatever form of discipline is given, much love is required. After a rebuke for bad behavior or a spanking for an unacceptable attitude, it is extremely important to affirm your love for that child. That doesn't mean go buy them a treat because you feel like a heel; give them a hug and lovingly explain what you expect from them. Be honest with them, and let them know you don't enjoy correcting them, but you do it because you love them. They may not understand it right away, but they will.

A Child's Smile & Three Little Words

I have cried a number of times since the birth of our first daughter. Like I said, I am an emotional man. I am not ashamed to admit that I cried during movies like *Armageddon* or *Rudy* or even *Sleepless in Seattle*. Some things just get to me. Like the first time I held her and realized she was real. Here was this gift from God, this blessing, and she was healthy and beautiful and perfect in every way. The emotions of those first few moments were overwhelming. My wife and I were parents for the first time. This was joy in its purest form. Our love had brought this incredible experience for us to share.

As they grow, your children will do many things that will disturb you. They will embarrass you from time to time, but don't worry; you can get back at them when they are teenagers. Don't focus on those things; deal with them and move on. You will have plenty of opportunities to embarrass one another from birth to adulthood.

I have this theory. Children have one mission in life, and that is to see what they can get! I believe the motivation of a child is not to make a parent proud, but to see how far they can push the boundaries set in place for their lives. Manipulation and blackmail are not off-limits; they are the tools with which a child expands their horizons. I need look no further than my youngest daughter to support my hypothesis.

Since the age of zero, my sweet, darling, angel of a child has had this innate, uncanny ability to use her cuteness to her advantage. It didn't get any better when she developed the ability to talk. At times, the words, "I love you, Daddy," have come across more like a threat than a statement. Well, not all the time, but occasionally.

Remember when you were a child? Didn't you give your parents numerous reasons to be mortified by your behavior? Well, maybe that was just me, but I know you got in trouble from time to time. You're not perfect, are you? I think of one time when my grandmother had taken me to the store. I was perfectly innocent, maybe four or five. I had no intentions of malicious behavior. I don't even remember the event. Apparently, I have blocked it from my memory because of its traumatic impact on my life. As Grandma pushed me through the aisles, I began to shout about one product in particular. Again, I must stress, I meant no harm. It wasn't my desire to embarrass my grandmother. As near as I can figure, I just recognized the item from an ad I had seen. I began to sing loudly, "Maxi pads, maxi pads," as my grandmother shushed me and tried to make it through the store without dying from embarrassment.

Those things will happen. I can remember many times when my children have said or done things that were more upsetting to me as a parent than they were to those around us who I was certain would be mortally offended by what they heard. In fact, it was more a fear of what they might think of me as a parent than concern for their own feelings. Kids will be kids, and they are bluntly honest. When they say something, they mean it, and they have no problems with sharing their opinion with an entire store full of strangers.

My children have embarrassed me. That's okay. I have pictures of them as babies in the tub that I will someday have the opportunity to share with others. It's a circle of life sort of thing. My children have also brought me to the brink of tears, not from embarrassment or laughter (though that has happened, too), but from their expression of love for their mother and me. Through words, pictures, cards and more, my children have shown their love for us, and not just so they could get something in return—though that has happened as well. I am talking about true, untarnished, unconditional love.

Is there anything more pure in the world than a child's love? Whether it's a hug when I am sad or a quick, "I love you, Daddy," on the way to the bus stop, it brightens my day. When one of our daughters smiles at me, it can make all the day's troubles disappear.

I remember crying the first time she said four simple little words: "I love you, Daddy." I have made it a point to let her know daily that I love her. As I have said before, even when she is in trouble and being disciplined, I reinforce that I love her and because of that, I cannot allow her to continue doing whatever it is she may have done.

I cannot think of anything that blesses my heart more than seeing my daughter's smile or hearing her laugh. One of my proudest moments as a father came from my daughter boldly proclaiming at her school that she wanted to be just like me someday. I wasn't there; I heard about it in a paper she wrote and from the teacher. She had nothing to gain from her statement. She said it because that was how she felt at that moment. Whatever she does, I will be proud of her. What she becomes is unimportant. Knowing that my girls can express their feelings freely without worrying about what others might think—that's what's important.

There will be times when a snuggling hug, a smile and the words, "I love you, Daddy," are meant to manipulate. I can handle that. I will always have those moments of unconditional love to cling to. I have held on to many of those things that have been written or drawn, and I will cherish the memory of those things that have been said. They are priceless and will be treasured for as long as I am able. I hope that my girls will always know how much I love them and that the memories I hold on to mean as much to them as they do to me.

Games Kids Play

Kids are so much fun! They have the ability to turn any situation into a game or any one thing into something fantastic. For some, that can be a source of joy; for others, frustration.

I don't know what happens to us when we graduate from high school or college, get married, work nine to five, pay bills, fix cars, find a better job, get a better car, buy a house … it's like when we have kids, we forget how to have fun.

For example, when I was younger, I used to amuse myself for hours with a tennis ball and a wall. I could play an entire nine-inning game of baseball by myself, bouncing the ball against the wall or a window. If I caught it, it was an out; if I missed it, depending on how far I had to run to get it, determined if it was a hit, double, home run, you get the idea. I wasn't bored; it was the World Series, and I was facing the meanest hitter the game had ever known. Sometimes, I would even strike him out.

Sure, I would have been mortified if one of my friends caught me; that's why it was all happening in my mind-every stat, every call by the announcer. That way, if anyone stopped by, I could just simply be playing catch. Have my mom walk up on that same situation, I'm pretty certain her response would be, "Hey, be careful, you're gonna break a window!"

Now, before you throw this book down and say to yourself, "This guy's nuts!" think back: you know somewhere in the back of your mind are memories of some silly game you used to play by yourself or with friends. That's what's great about kids; they can amuse themselves in almost any situation.

Being an adult can be overwhelming, but it's not the child's fault. More often than we realize, our kids would rather have us and the box that the expensive gift we worked three extra shifts to afford than the toy itself. I think we as adults need things to hold our attention so we assume that kids are the same way, but they're not. They still have imagination. They still have curiosity. They still have dreams.

You are adequate. Before you ask yourself, "*What?*" hear me out. I think we try to make up for our self-perceived shortcomings as parents through the things we give our kids. Like, to your child, just spending time with you wouldn't be enough; we trick ourselves into believing they need something more. Don't believe me; look at this comparison.

We took our girls to a fancy amusement park with the huge rollercoasters and a licensed character area with some of their favorite television shows represented. We had a great time and made lots of memories, but I don't know who the trip meant more to: them or me. I look back in my mind at the joy I saw in them at the high-dollar amusement complex and realized it wasn't any different than the joy they had when we go to the local park and play together on the jungle gym or when we go fishing together or on a picnic. It just cost more.

Kids are content sitting in a high chair, taking a ring of plastic keys and throwing them on the floor over and over again. They will style your hair (if you have any), play with dolls or action figures or cars, play hide and seek, anything; but it's even better if you play, too.

I'm not saying don't go on vacations to far-off places where incredible memories are made; do that, but be there in between the big stuff. Don't be afraid to act like a kid; it won't affect your ability to be relevant to your child, it will enhance it.

And sure, sometimes those games that kids play get a little annoying. They might not hold your interest like screaming down the first hill of a huge rollercoaster or football on the TV, but it's not about you! It's all about the children!

Girls Will Be Boys; Well, Not Really

One of the biggest challenges of being the father of two beautiful little girls has been to not raise them as little boys. I am a red-blooded, all-American male. I like football, hockey, racing, fishing, hunting... you get the idea. Face it, if there is a chance something is going to get hit, there is fighting involved or things go really fast, I like it! I grunt and burp with the best of them. I love to compete. If you are better at something than I am, I will do everything I can to improve in that area so I can beat you! I like to win. I won't cheat to win, but I will use every advantage available to improve my chances within the limit of the rulebook. I am not above using intimidation tactics while playing. I am a big man and that can be a great help during times of battle. How am I supposed to raise two girls?

I want them to be competitive. I want them to know that there are winners and losers in all situations in life, and that losing makes you stronger. I want them to realize that failure is not bad; not trying for fear of losing is. I don't want them to get an "A" because everyone else did. I want them to get an "A" because they did the work necessary to achieve an "A." Achievement builds character and discipline. There are too many undisciplined people with a shelf full of trophies in this world; my girls will know what it's like to lose.

One of the best ways to learn about winning and losing is through sports. There is nothing wrong with a girl who likes sports. I like to think that one day a young man will come to my door, having passed through intense screening procedures, to ask for my daughter's hand in marriage. After I grill him intensely while sharpening my broadheads, if he still makes the cut, I believe he will thank me from the bottom of his heart that I have raised two young women that love sports, like to camp, can fish, belch and shoot with the best of them. In my mind I see him weeping, and that's okay. As I have established before, real men cry.

My girls like to wrestle, watch NASCAR and go to Arena Football games. It occurred to me one day (my wife may take credit for this, but believe me, I came to this realization on my own) that, though being able to burp the entire alphabet in one incredible belch is a talent that might take you far, it's not the most appealing trait in a little girl.

Little girls should be refined. They should play dress-up and have tea parties. They should dream about princes and far-away kingdoms where they will live happily ever after. They should know that you think they are beautiful and will love them no matter what. They need to know that they are your princesses. It builds their self-esteem and creates a bond between father and daughter that is nearly unbreakable. But there is nothing wrong with a girl fishing with her daddy. There has to be a balance.

I remember the girls in school who were so unsure of themselves. There were two extremes: tomboys who were easy to spot, and the girls who hated everything about themselves and were harder to detect. I don't ever want my daughters to feel as though they have to earn my love. I don't want them to feel that they aren't good enough just as God made them. Now I don't believe that every problem a child has can be attributed and blamed solely on the parents, but a child's self-confidence is dependent upon the love of a father.

It would have been nice to have had a little boy, but I have been incredibly blessed with two of the most beautiful girls God has ever created. It is a privilege and an honor to play dolls with them. I have had just as much fun watching their favorite show on ice as I have had with them at a race. It may not be my favorite thing to do, but as long as I am with my favorite people, where we are isn't nearly as important as the fact that we are together.

It is a balance that requires sacrifice and a willingness to be humiliated (trust me, there's nothing like having unexpected guests just after your daughters decided to do your hair and put every clip they owned on your head), but it's worth it. I'm not just raising a little girl; I am developing character in her that she will look for in someone else. In that, I can be confident that when she does bring someone home, he will be someone who respects her and values her for who she is. She will be confident enough to know that she doesn't have to be something or someone she isn't just to be loved. That is worth a million tea parties or a hundred embarrassing moments. They are my princesses, and I want the best for them. Honestly, it's because I selfishly want the best for them that I am willing to invest myself to such a degree. There will still be problems. There will be growing pains. There will be heartbreak, but when that happens, I know where they will turn and I will be there, waiting to help them grow.

Please Don't Eat the Kitty

You wouldn't think it would be necessary, but if you have children and you have pets, eventually your child will try to eat one of them, and you will hear yourself say, "Stop biting the cat!" Don't be alarmed; this is natural. When a child sees just about anything, they will put it in their mouth eventually. That's why many toys are labeled for children three and older. (I assume that label is there for the adult, because I can't tell you how many times my girls have asked for stuff that wasn't age appropriate. It's like young children can't read or something!)

I can think of a number of occasions when one of the girls would grab a handful of the dog's hair and pull with all their might. Thankfully, though the dog didn't seem overjoyed at this activity, she tolerated it. (Yes, the dog is a girl, too! We've had two cats, both girls! Go figure!) The dog, who we affectionately named Pickles, would look at me as if to say, "You gonna do something about this?"

They would kiss the dog, too. It looked like they were getting ready to take a bite out of a big old steak. Mouth open, drool dripping, they would place whatever they could reach in their mouth. The tail, the back, the snout, which in turn would be greeted by a lashing of slimy dog tongue, which always grosses me out cause all I can think of is, *You just cleaned your butt with that, get it off my kid!*

Let me give you a little advice about pets and kids. Stick with fish; they're easier to replace when they die. You can do it without the child even realizing the fish is different. You see one goldfish, you've seen them all. However, if you must have something larger than an aquatic pet, stick with a dog. I like cats, but cats aren't nearly as forgiving and tolerant as a dog.

When a child runs and jumps and "accidentally" lands on the dog, more often than not, the dog might yelp, then move and find another place that is safer to lie in. Same scenario, but replace the dog with a cat. Kitty gets indignant, scratches at the child, hisses, maybe even bites. Daddy gets mad, throws cat across living room. Not a good situation.

When a child gives doggy a kiss, typically the worst that happens is child receives a tongue bath from doggy. No problem; saves you a step, they needed a bath anyway, right? Trade places with kitty and you end up giving your child the Heimlich because they're gagging from a hairball.

Not to mention, children are inquisitive, and a litter box can look like a day at the beach to the unsuspecting child. No, cats can be funny. Sometimes they can even be loving, but if you want a pet that's child-ready, a dog's probably the best bet. They may make a mess in the yard, but at least you won't have to worry about your child eating "chocolates" from kitty's sand box.

Teach Them While They're Teachable

(Use Them While They're Willing)

Let's get serious for a minute. Believe it or not, you are the biggest influence on your child's life. I know; sometimes it doesn't seem like it, but trust me, you are. You will shape their moral values, their work ethic and their relational skills more than any other influencing force in their lives. You will teach them far more than they learn from their friends, from their teachers or from the influence of media outlets. That is, you will if you make a point of engaging them on a daily basis. Get involved! Don't sit on the sidelines and let people who don't share your values be a greater influence than you are.

As children and pre-teens, they will depend on you for everything. You will be their hero who can do no wrong. When they are teenagers, they will need you to be there to guide them through the transition to adulthood. You will influence them in ways you may never realize until they become adults. Many parents make the mistake of trying to give their kids space. Your teenagers will need you just as much as a teen if not more than they did as a child. They may act like you annoy them. They may tell you that you are weird. But when the chips are down, when it really matters, they'll turn to you.

You may be thinking, *What does he know? His kids aren't teens!* and you would be correct; but I am not just a parent, I am also a youth pastor and have been for sixteen years. Whether I have been volunteering or a paid staff member, I have seen tendencies in students that have held true regardless of age, sex, race, or economic status. I can quickly tell whose parents are involved and whose are disengaged. Being brought up in poor conditions doesn't guarantee a child will grow to become a criminal just as being wealthy isn't a free pass to functioning normally as an adult. The only thing that's certain is that children whose parents are a part of their lives daily are less likely to struggle in any number of areas.

There have been times as a parent that I have made mistakes. I have lost my temper and corrected my child harshly. I have yelled at my girls and had to apologize afterwards. Undoubtedly, you will, too. It doesn't make you a bad parent. Parenting is a lifelong learning curve. Some days you'll be ahead of the curve, on other days you will lag behind. The only thing that would make you a bad parent is an unwillingness to try. Failure is a lack of trying for fear of an undesired outcome.

In order to teach, two things need to be present: a student—in this case, your child—trusting that, as their teacher, you will instruct them in the proper course of action, and a teacher who is willing to invest a part of themselves in the life of that student. Teaching requires action and a willingness to become a part of the life being taught, no matter how trivial the task. Take housework for example.

Our children are willing to help clean house. Being young, sometimes the help becomes more of a chore, but my job is to teach them, and willing people are teachable. Teaching isn't always easy, but it is necessary. I can't expect anyone to perform a task I set them to the way I want them to do it if I am not willing to try and teach them whether they are a child or an adult. Right now, my children want to make me proud by helping around the house and, for the time, I will let them. They don't realize that I am developing a standard in their lives that will stay with them forever. By allowing a child to help with the dishes or the laundry, I am teaching them a skill and it is much easier to teach a child who wants to help than to force a child who for years was told they weren't old enough to perform what I am now demanding that they accomplish.

It isn't always easy. Sometimes the laundry soap gets spilled or the floor has to be swept twice. That's okay. Use this time to teach them the way to do things. They are willing, and there is a lot to be done, so use them. My girls and I have a great time cleaning house each week and that may not last for long, but I am going to do everything I can to teach them while they are teachable. The only way I fail as a parent is if I don't try.

Take A Little Time

I learned the hard way that you have to take a little time for yourself. Face it, you spend your entire day watching kids' shows, playing kid games and having kid conversations; you need a break! It's not a selfish thing. When you find yourself in a room full of adults who are having general discussions about things like the price of gas or the state of the economy, you're gonna need a little something more to fall back on than the wisdom of a little red puppet, no matter how cute he is.

It dawned on me one day that, other than my wife, there were times that I had no interaction with adults, aside from church. Now, I love my wife, but we could sit and talk for hours about what the girls were learning or doing. I got to a point where I felt like I couldn't talk with adults; they just didn't make sense.

It got to a point where some friends even told my wife and I that we needed to get away from the girls for a night. When you have people volunteering to watch your kids so you can go out, take advantage of it! (Use wisdom, of course. Don't leave your kids with someone prone to sleeping twenty-three hours a day. If you feel uncomfortable leaving your child with an individual, don't. You won't enjoy the time you have together because you'll be worried about your kids the whole time.)

Here's a little quiz for you and your spouse to take. Answer the questions truthfully because you will be graded. Just kidding, this is a book. However, I guarantee that how you score on the test will be directly reflected in your relationship. Here goes!

If you are blessed with the opportunity to go on a date (with your spouse, focus!) do you go out for a romantic dinner, look each other in the eyes and talk about your future and your life together, or do you look around, feeling awkward because there isn't anyone tugging on your pant leg asking you if they can go to the play-place? Or, do you make the mistake we made and decide to go out for a romantic dinner and take the kids with you? Trust me, this just doesn't work! They cry, you cry. They scream, you rip out your hair and question whether your child is the victim of possession.

You stand at the movie theater, holding hands, trying to decide which movie you will watch. You have no children with you, so you don't have to consider the kiddy films, but you find yourself drawn to those cute little animated characters. Do you try to regain your composure and look for the best option that is age appropriate but doesn't put your witness at risk, or do you smile at each other, make up some excuse about making sure it's okay for the kids, and politely ask the kid at the counter for two tickets to the latest fairytale adaptation of princes and princesses frolicking in the prairie? Stop laughing; I'm serious. If it hasn't happened, it will! What will you do?

You're walking through the mall, kids all around, except yours who are safe at home with the babysitter. You walk along talking about your love for one another and how every moment together is better than the one before, or each time you start to discuss each other, you're distracted by a window display of Barbie dolls or Disney princesses? Really, my wife and I were away celebrating our 10th anniversary, a state away from our babies, and the first few days of the getaway looked more like an advance team deployed to scout out the terrain for future visits with the kids. We would find ourselves shopping for them and talking about how much they would enjoy the places we went. We had the same thought at the same time. We looked at each other and said, "We've got to stop!"

Now, hear me out, thinking about your kids isn't bad. Spending a little time shopping for them while you're together is okay. However, if you can't focus on one another because all you have to talk about is your kids, it's time for a break!

Your relationship with your spouse is the single most important relationship you have with another human being. That relationship needs nurturing. It needs focus time, where you allow yourselves to only talk about each other. It doesn't make you a bad parent. It makes you a better parent. You will know one another, intimately. Your love for each other will continue to grow, and your kids will see a proper husband and wife relationship, something we see very little of on television or in society today.

You have to make sure that you take time to talk with your friends; you know, the ones you hung out with before the kids. And don't dominate the conversation with "My kids did this" and "Oh, they are just so cute" topics! Talk about your kids, but talk about other things, too. Be interested in your friend. It won't be long and you'll feel like an adult again.

Some danger signs to look out for include, but are not limited to: looking forward to new videos coming out only when Disney has a new release; eating out is limited to places that ask, "Would you like fries with that?"; or, sitting with friends, you find yourself discussing the new Barney video as the last movie you watched. Also, if you find yourself talking baby talk with the pastor at church, you may need a little you time.

You're not selfish. You just need a break. If you don't watch for the warning signs, you won't even realize what's happening. One day, you'll just realize, as you lounge in your Barney t-shirt and your SpongeBob boxers, that you can't remember the last time you had a conversation with an adult that didn't include kids movies, the latest toy that everyone has to have or how many new things your child has learned that amaze you. Seriously, you can revert so badly that you begin to be bitter towards your kids, and that's not good. Take a little time and focus on yourself and your wife. Your kids will thank you for it.

Joint Responsibility for Mom & Dad

No matter the situation, husbands and wives should share in the household responsibilities. If you are the spouse who is working outside the home, this chapter is especially for you. No one should feel like they are missing something because they are home caring for their children. There is no greater responsibility as a parent than the welfare of our kids.

For the spouse who has spent the day at work, this isn't going to make any sense. In fact, it will seem completely irrational, but that doesn't change the fact that this next statement is completely true. After a long day of caring for children, cooking, cleaning and whatever else might arise (see "Diapers Should Come with Super Glue Tabs"), there can be very real jealousy and bitterness towards the spouse who gets to go out and interact with other adults each day.

It is irrational, but a few days at home with minimal adult contact can make the nine-to-five life look appealing. It can look like a vacation. One of the last things that the stay-at-home parent wants to hear about is how their husband or wife had to go and hear a boring presentation followed by lunch with their coworkers where they talked about paperwork and the office scene. *That sounds like heaven,* they think, *and you're complaining.*

Remember this: the most intelligent and stimulating conversation that your spouse may have had that day started with a question like, "Why can't I stuff beans up my nose?" or, "Why does it hurt when I do this?" Maybe they spent the day explaining to that darling child that they cannot put on a cape and expect to fly from the roof. They may have even had to explain that human children cannot grow up to become talking tomatoes or a cat. (Then again, with the scientific advancements, I guess anything is possible).

It can come to a point of resentment between Mom and Dad. That's why it is extremely important for you to listen intently to each other. You may be the only human adult contact for your spouse through the course of the day unless you count people who have cartoon animals for pets or live in a house full of puppets and trolleys.

Look for the warning signs. Things like dressing from head to toe in purple velvet or wearing shirts that only have thick horizontal stripes; if you notice this kind of behavior, take the kids and give your significant other a little private time for their sanity's sake—not to mention the health of the children and yourself.

Some things that will go a long way towards keeping a healthy balance include helping with the house work, bring home dinner on occasion and make time for each other.

I cannot stress that part enough! Take time to build upon the relational foundations that lead from marriage to having children. Your love life shouldn't suffer or be put on hold because of the pitter patter of little feet. Little feet have to sleep from time to time. If you help each other with the household chores or pitch in from time to time with the kids, energy will be available for other things that might not have been if help wasn't offered.

Joint responsibility applies to more than just housework, dinner, or an occasional break from the madness that is child-rearing. It includes changing diapers and disciplining your child. By the way, watching the kids so your spouse can run out to buy groceries or diapers doesn't count as giving them a break. It is a good way to get something thrown at your head.

Often, the stay-at-home spouse can be guilty of using the threat of, "Just wait until later. You'll be in so much trouble when Mom or Dad gets home!" You're not doing yourself any favors by not taking charge of the situation at hand. Don't put off disciplining for poor behavior unless you feel that you are going to lose control. Don't make your children fret and fear their father or mother.

Let me make this extremely simple. Whether you are the spouse who works outside the house or the stay-at-home mom or dad, put yourself in the place of your spouse when you face dilemmas. You wouldn't like it if you came home with the weight of the day on you and discovered that you had been deemed executioner of necessary punishment rather than a hug from your kids. In the same way, if you had been home all day, you wouldn't appreciate having your spouse come in and say things like, "The house is a wreck," or, "Here, the kid needs to be changed; I gotta go and watch some TV."

It's all about compromise. The couple that learns to work together and compliment each other, verbally and physically, that's the couple that will raise great kids. Share the load so the weight doesn't become too much to bear. You will establish a lifelong characteristic of service in your children if they see you tripping over yourselves to help each other.

Your kids will look to the example of Mom and Dad. They will follow it, and one day they will look for those qualities in their own spouse. A little further down the road of life, they will fall back on those things they learned from you as they raise their own children. The cycle will continue. Serve each other without expectation of getting something in return. See the value in what each spouse brings to the marriage. You both are responsible and are an intricate part in a sacred covenant. Why would you want to do anything to hurt that? Be willing to do whatever it takes to fulfill your duty as a parent, as a spouse and, most important of all, a child of God.

I Love It So Much

(I Work With Other People's Kids, Too!)

Not only do I take care of my own children, I am also a youth pastor. I have served as a volunteer and as full-time paid staff. It is an honor to have the call of God on my life, but it can present some significant challenges in the area of family. I am currently on staff at a church where I have served as youth pastor for over six years. Throughout that time, I have had to balance time with my youth kids and time with my children.

Balancing areas of our lives is not as difficult as we make it. As a youth pastor, I have placed unreasonable expectations upon myself and on those around me. It's in those moments that my life as a parent is out of balance. I believe that God honors our efforts when we set our priorities according to his plan, not our own. I cannot measure my success by the size of my youth ministry or by the number of families I have helped bring into our church. My success is determined by a different set of ideals.

You may not be a youth minister, but you are a human being. Each one of us has to set our lives along similar priorities. If we don't, we will always feel as though something is missing. My family is second only to my personal walk with God. After God comes my wife, then my children, then others, including my calling as a youth pastor. I have to put myself somewhere after all these other things, or I will never feel contentment like the Apostle Paul speaks of in his letters.

My girls are a part of nearly everything I do as a youth minister. They are with me on outings and at the church (when they aren't in school). When I am at a camp, they get to go on vacation with their grandparents, and they love it! We have a very busy life. We have to follow a schedule and then be flexible enough to make changes when someone is sick or a student is in trouble.

My success is measured by this: when my girls are grown, that they have not turned from the faith my wife and I have been teaching them. I have seen too many families in ministry where the children feel resentment toward church. My hope and desire is that our girls love the Lord as adults like they do now. Only time will tell, but I am doing things in an effort to see that, as a father, I do nothing that would cause them to turn away.

When my children have events at school, I am there. My church family knows that my first priority is my own family. I have been blessed with a pastor who supports this line of thinking and encourages it.

He is active in the lives of his children, and he expects me to be a part of what's going on at my daughters' school. We have set family times that would take an act of God to change. I protect those times, and I do my best to make the most of every opportunity that I am given.

My students know where I stand. They know my priorities, and I hope they respect me because I have been up-front with them. I am showing my children what it means to be a father, and I am also showing a group of teenagers who look at my life and then measure what I have said against what I do to see if the result is what I told them it would be. If my family was out-of-whack, and my children hated me and the ministry and my wife resented what I do, then I would not be successful.

If I have the largest youth ministry in the state and our church is growing because our youth are on fire for God but my family suffers, then nothing else I accomplish matters. My first responsibility is to my wife and children. I can't be a father to all the teens I encounter, but I can make an impact on their lives by doing what I believe to be right. I can say these things until I turn blue. They mean nothing unless I live them.

You may not be a youth minister or a Sunday school teacher. You may not even go to church (I hope you do, and if you don't, now might be the time to start), but you are more than just a parent. Your identity is made up of more than just what you are a part of at that moment. Your worth comes from within you and through the knowledge that Christ died for you. You are not just a businessman, a shop owner or a doctor. You are not just a mother or a father. You are God's creation and you have purpose beyond what you do.

What drives me is to know that someday, if I have done my job right, my children will teach my grandchildren the same things I am teaching them today. In my ministry, I want to be more than a youth pastor. I want to be an example of how things can be if you will put your family first. Like I said before, we may not have the newest things the day they come out. Our home may not be the biggest and our cars may have some rust, but our lives will be filled with the only thing that brings true happiness: love.

Whether I am paid for what I do or I am a volunteer, whether we have or we lack, as long as we have each other, there is nothing we cannot overcome. We have a Father who cares for us more than we can comprehend. Happiness isn't found in things. It's found in family, friends, and knowing that you are loved. You can drive around in a beat-up old Chevette that's missing the floor panels and might not get you from point "a" to point "b" without a stop at point "c," but if you're with the ones you love, you're creating memories that will outlast that car. I would like to think that I have impacted the lives of my students in ways that will outlast their possessions. I would like to live a life worth imitating. Then I will have achieved success and balance. Then I will be content.

When you really examine it and you look at your life, you will see that you have so much more than you might have gained from a job that pays you millions. You haven't cheated yourself at all; your life is fuller, and you find that you want for nothing. That is balance, and that's the key to happiness. You could search a million lives and find that being truly happy and wanting for nothing has little to do with a person's income or social status. The ones who are truly happy find a way to work through every situation, keeping their focus on what's important: God, family, friends, work, and self. Without that balance, something will always be missing.

Now if I can just make it through the teenage years! God bless!